NEGOTIATING
the Deal

Also by Kerry Johnson

NEGOTIATING
the Deal

KERRY JOHNSON MBA, Ph.D.

MEDIA

Published 2022 by Gildan Media LLC
aka G&D Media
www.GandDmedia.com

FIRST EDITION 2022

Front cover design by David Rheinhardt of Pyrographx

Interior design by Meghan Day Healey of Story Horse, LLC

Library of Congress Cataloging-in-Publication Data is available upon request

ISBN: 978-1-7225-0185-3

10 9 8 7 6 5 4 3 2 1

To my first grandson, James Lincoln
You will be a great negotiator.
Your parents will help you become a pro.
You will get all that you want if you work hard
and love your family and our Lord God.
Remember to negotiate for what you want.
Your grandparents love you to the moon and back.

Contents

Introduction

D o you negotiate? Do you know how to negotiate? Most people say no. Many think prices are set in stone. They often pay whatever the sticker shows. Yet it's not only car prices that can be negotiated.

One of my golf buddies, Anthony, was able to negotiate a rental agreement for an apartment recently. The seller wanted $1,750 a month. Anthony offered $1,400 while making the case he was stable and had a history of making rental payments on time. He also introduced pressure on the seller by saying that a competing apartment manager was offering $1,200 a month at roughly the same square footage. The landlord accepted the $1,400 without making a counteroffer.

Negotiation is often about price discovery. It is also about more than just money. Perhaps the landlord had to evict a tenant in the past and didn't want to go through that again. Perhaps they were tired of the marketing and advertising expense. Whatever the reason, Anthony's negotiation skills came in handy. The landlord might have leased the apartment for less than $1,400. We will never know, since there was no counteroffer.

Negotiation Is the Most Money You Will Ever Make

The truth is that you negotiate every day, especially outside of work. But when you negotiate within your job, the time spent negotiating is the most profitable you will ever engage in. Let that sink in. By learning the skills in this book, you will make more money per hour by negotiating than by any other income producing activity.

Let's assume that your income is $100,000 a year. Based on a normal 2,000 hours worked in a year, your income is $50 per hour. Let's also assume that you want to buy a used car that costs $20,000. Because of your masterful negotiation skills, you're able to purchase it for $18,000. The negotiation took one hour of your time. The effort earned you $2,000 per hour. Looks pretty good, doesn't it?

You will make even more money on larger agreements. Most will refinance their mortgage every 3.5 years. They will purchase and sell a home every seven years. Let's also assume your home is $750,000. The seller's market of 2021 notwithstanding, you will probably need to negotiate. We also assume that you don't expect the home to sell for more than $700,000. But in the end, an enthusiastic buyer gives you $725,000. That is $25,000 more than you expected to get. That also means that a three-hour negotiation produced a return of $25,000. You can make the case that your negotiation skills made you $8,000 per hour.

What if you wanted to buy a house listed for $750,000? Anything less than that would be a success. In a buyer's market, Realtors love to brag that they can typically buy for 10 percent below the listing price. Let's assume that is overly optimistic, and only 5 percent below listing is possible. That still means your negotiation skills made you nearly $38,000. Depending on how many hours the actual negotiation took, your time is now worth more than $13,000 per hour. But only when you negotiate.

You will make more money per hour on a single negotiation than in any other activity. So why haven't you taken a course on negotiation? If this is the most lucrative hourly activity you will ever engage in, why wing it?

What Is Your Time Worth?

Many people think negotiating a better deal is not worth the time. They don't want to go to the effort, and they think it's awkward and embarrassing. Is it really worth it to get another $100 off the price? Is it worth it to get a 50 percent discount on a vacation? Is it worth it to negotiate a medical plan with zero deductible instead of $1,500 a year as is the case with most?

The real question, though, is, how much is your time worth? Let's say you make $60 an hour. If you can negotiate a $300 discount in five minutes, is it worth it? If you can use a technique known as the vise (which I'll go into later) to get an extra one-week paid vacation, is it worth it? Let's say you make $10,000 a month. An extra week vacation is worth $2,500. Your time is worth $60 an hour. That means to make $2,500, you will have to work nearly 42 hours. Is the effort expended in using the vise worth 42 hours of your time?

This is how you need to think about negotiation. If you are making $10,000 a month and working towards a deal will benefit you less than $60, just accept the offer. But any activity worth more than $60 an hour is a very good use of your time. If you can learn these techniques, you can negotiate with anybody, any time, for anything. You will never make money faster in any endeavor in your life then when you negotiate.

Children are the best negotiators. My daughters would harangue me until they got their way. Of course, their skill set was limited, but they'd never give up. Children are better negotiators than adults because they are less concerned about looking foolish or being rejected. They simply focus on what they want and do whatever they can to get it. This is the attitude adults need to develop. If you could gain a child's focus on getting what they want, remember these skills, and add elegance to the conversation, you could produce much better outcomes.

The Negotiation You Never Want to Have

When she was twenty years old, my youngest daughter, Caroline, attended an awards dinner as my date. We were celebrating one of my tennis tournament wins. At the end of the event, she left separately at 9:15 p.m. I left at 9:30. On the way home, I passed an ambulance on the 55 freeway in Costa Mesa, California. I felt bad for the person they were rescuing.

The ambulance was for my daughter. Caroline was hit by a drunk driver that evening. The girl that smashed into her Chevy Volt was going 125 mph with a blood alcohol level of .24, three times the legal limit. She hit Caroline's front fender, backed off, and then hit her left rear fender, sending Caroline's Volt careening off the freeway down an 85-foot embankment, end over end, and hitting a tree.

As I pulled into the driveway at home, I received a phone call from the California Highway Patrol reporting that my daughter was in an accident and that I should come to the Western Medical Center. I was there in only a few minutes. As I entered the waiting area, I could hear my daughter screaming with pain. Entering the trauma room, I put my arm around her, which immediately gave her comfort and quiet. She had multiple bruises and lacerations. The gas pedal had penetrated her right foot. Other damage was a severe concussion producing headaches, anxiety, an inability to focus, and insomnia. This lasted for nearly two years and caused her to drop out of college to convalesce.

A very good friend, an Orange County Superior Court judge, recommended a personal injury attorney. At first, they said the compensation would be limited since there was no major physical damage. They encouraged me to settle for only $13,000, saying any more compensation would be difficult to get. I pushed them to keep negotiating with Farmers Insurance Company, which, coincidentally, was also my insurance company. The negotiation went on for more than a year. The attorneys continually pushed to close the case, while I refused to accept any settlement that I thought was unfair. I didn't know how long her psychological trauma would last, or the extent of her medical bills.

I soon realized this nationally known personal injury firm really only wanted to deal with cases promising settlements in the hundreds of thousands, if not millions, of dollars. For them, further negotiation was not worth their time. But a settlement for your daughter is worth negotiating as long as it takes to get compensated for the injury to her future. We eventually settled for $50,000, quadrupling the first offer. The attorney assigned to my case would talk to me frequently. I encouraged the attorney to use many of the techniques and skills you are learning in this book.

This is how we need to think about negotiation. Is it worth the time expended? Is it worth the distraction from other things you could be working on? That is your decision. It shouldn't take a child's injury to cause us to apply negotiation skills. As I found, my advocacy was critical in making sure the personal injury firm didn't just cut their loss of time and quit. My knowledge of negotiation helped me create a better outcome for my daughter.

You can use negotiation in everything you do: sports, business, and even with your kids. The more you use these techniques, the more comfortable you will be, and the more effective you will become.

Why Don't We All Negotiate?

The reason is that many of us find it uncomfortable. We think of it as nitpicky and awkward. We just hope the prices listed are the lowest possible based on competitive pressure. We assume buyers and sellers will generally be fair. We assume a good deal without the rigor of negotiating. Why risk rejection? Why risk a feeling of failure if the other side doesn't want to negotiate?

In fact, many people think it's embarrassing to negotiate, even disparaging the process as "haggling." Recently, a company president in San Diego asked me to speak at four client events. The president asked what my speaking fee was. Was there was a discount for four presentations? I said yes and offered to stay within their budget. He then asked again for my discount price. Not wanting to make the first offer, I repeated that I would stay within his budget. We spoke for a few more minutes about his past speakers and how they decreased their fees. But I would not budge. Exacerbated, he said, "I'm very uncomfortable haggling over price." Disingenuously, I agreed and asked what would make him comfortable. He then finally told me his budget, to which I countered. Finally, we reached an agreement.

This is representative of many people who aren't accustomed to negotiation. Many of my clients enjoy it. They have fun. They use it in every facet of life. They negotiate price, delivery speed, and even extras when they buy products and services.

Negotiation Is Already a Part of Your Life

I'm a 15.8-handicap golfer and constantly have to negotiate bets with other golfers on the first tee. Personally, I'd be just as happy playing a relaxed round, but my friends always want to bet. Golfers really don't want to be cheap, but male golfers have healthy egos and don't like to lose. So if you don't effectively negotiate strokes on the first tee, you're going to lose and be annoyed the whole round, especially when it comes to coming up with dough at the end. I am so used to this first-tee ritual that I now flinch, bracket, and use the vise (techniques I'll be describing later).

The best golfer in the group usually wants to play straight up, without giving strokes. One player says he hasn't played in three months, while another claims injury. One player is unfamiliar with the course; another says he doesn't feel well. All of this is a game to get strokes, and a negotiated settlement is always the outcome. While this is fun, few realize they are negotiating. Even more fail to understand that while negotiation won't help their golf game, it will lessen the impact on their pocketbook if they lose the bet.

When my brother Kevin says, "Let's play straight up," I tell him my handicap is 20. He will say, "I thought you said your handicap was 10." Then we bracket to 15, very close to my 15.8, making it much fairer. A few weeks ago, my buddies only offered to give me only 6 strokes instead of 10. I flinched, saying, "You'll have to do better than that." They all laughed and said, "You're using those stupid negotiation techniques again, aren't you?" Eventually they gave up and just asked how many strokes I wanted

Without even knowing it, you negotiate multiple times every day. If you organize a time for a follow-up phone call, completion dates with your boss, yardwork with your wife, or even how much allowance to give your kids, you are negotiating.

If you are at a restaurant and hear the wait is over an hour, it can be tempting to leave. But a good negotiator might ask to sit at the bar until the hostess has a no-show. Since you are at the restaurant anyway, it might be more convenient for the host to just call you over instead of taking the time to contact the next person on the waiting list.

Perhaps your airline flight cancels because of a mechanical failure. The gate agent is willing to put you on a flight two days from now, because the next flight is fully booked. A good negotiator might ask instead to be put on standby on a flight two hours later. The agent assures you won't make the flight. But when you approach the new gate agent, you say your flight was canceled. You will also be close to the podium in case a confirmed passenger doesn't show up.

Finally, your sales manager asks to increase sales for the quarter to make up for low production from other colleagues. Of course, you will gain extra commission money. But instead, you request a week's vacation pay if you can meet the increased objective. The sales manager is able to hit his goals. You are able to achieve yours.

These examples are all about your ability to negotiate. Every day is the same. You negotiate without even knowing it. The real skill and elegance of negotiation is making the other side feel they have won. It may be tempting to get a better deal from a desperate buyer or seller. In fact, they may have to take your offer because they have no other choice.

This book is not about a win-lose negotiation style. It's not about getting a good deal at all costs. It's about getting the deal you want while also preserving relationships. When you build and strengthen relationships, your career will also steadily progress. It's about making sure that we continue to achieve outcomes that benefit both sides.

Negotiating at the Berlin Wall

In 1989, my then girlfriend and soon to be wife, Merita, and I went to Frankfurt, Germany, for a speech. It was my thirty-fifth birthday, which we celebrated over champagne. After my presentation the next day, one of the attendees said the Berlin Wall was falling—a historic event. That evening, Merita and I bought tickets to Berlin departing the next morning.

The wall was being sledge-hammered and dismantled by thousands of Germans and tourists on both sides. Demo tools were selling for triple the price. I have pieces of the Berlin wall in my desk at home. Perhaps the East German revenge was constructing the wall out of asbestos, so it would be toxic to anybody handling it.

The next day, we arranged a tour through East Berlin. West Berlin was vibrant, colorful, and modern. East Berlin was gray, poorly maintained, and impoverished. The East Berlin tour guide met our bus on the west side near Checkpoint Charlie. Her first diatribe was to tell us the faults and inequities of capitalism. She went on for nearly twenty minutes discussing how unfair capitalism was to workers, families, and anybody who was not ultrawealthy.

During the three-hour tour, the guide took us through factories, museums and even one shop selling wooden handmade toy trains. The price was in East German marks, with the set exchange rate of three East German marks to one West German mark. I knew I could get a better deal from one of the exchange shops close by. I asked the tour guide where the closest exchange shop was. She immediately volunteered to exchange my West German marks. I asked what her rate was, and she said three to one. I then said I could get eight to one anywhere else. (This is called *competition pressure*—another tactic I'll explore in this book.) When she offered nine East German marks for one West German mark, I accepted.

Ironically, this lifelong communist, who hated capitalism, was so willing to engage in it. She negotiated without even knowing it. I speak German. I facetiously asked her if she enjoyed engaging in a capitalist deal. She denied that we were. She refused to accept that we were doing anything except helping each other. She said she was trying to help a tour customer buy a wooden train.

What You Will Learn from This Book

Many books on negotiation discuss mechanics, techniques, skills, and tactics. But this is the first book ever written on applying psychology and advanced communication to the negotiation process. For example, would it be helpful if you knew whether the other side was telling the truth? Would it benefit you if you could see a buying signal? It would prevent you from overpresenting and could help you gain concessions more quickly.

What if you could use a simple five-step listening technique to discover the other side's goals? Would this help you to achieve your own goals? Negotiation is not only about gambits, it's about people. People communicate emotionally as well as logically. Negotiation skills are not only a matter of logic; they are also based on psychology, emotion, fear, and dreams. This book goes to a higher level in the negotiation process to help you achieve the outcomes you want.

There are specific skills that will make any negotiation more successful. Just like learning a language, these steps need to be both learned and remembered. Some of these skills are as simple as *never make a first offer*. The price of a product or service is only what both parties are willing to agree on. If you make a first offer, you never know what the seller is willing to accept, only what you are willing to buy it for.

Another basic skill you will learn is to *never split the difference*. Negotiators who are uncomfortable and have poor skills accept anything in the middle. In this case, you both can agree on a price. But you will never know what the seller is willing to accept.

We will discuss many other basic negotiation skills that will enable you to get a good deal in any negotiation. We will also discuss how to handle more difficult negotiations. For example, how would you overcome an impasse? How would you cope with an unenthusiastic seller or buyer? How would you cope with a negotiation partner who has to bring your offer up to a committee? This is one of most difficult types of negotiation you will ever encounter. Since you have to communicate with the committee through an intermediary, you may not know what is important to the decision makers or what they want to achieve.

We will also talk about advanced negotiation techniques. Sometimes a certain outcome may be more important than money. For example, a car dealership may want to achieve the highest margin possible in the beginning of the month, but feels pressure to make better deals at the end of the month. Perhaps there is a push for warranties from the manufacturer that the dealer wants even more than the price of the car.

There may also be the occasion where one department has reached its budget. They might even say your price is too high. Another department may still have funds that can be used for your product or service. You would not know that unless you knew what to ask.

Many books on negotiation discuss skills and steps as well as providing case study illustrations. Here you are reading about negotiation from a psychological standpoint. We will go much deeper in building communication skills that will help you in any negotiation. We will talk about how to gain trust during negotiation. We will discuss how to discover when your negotiation partner is telling the truth or lying. According to FBI studies and research from the University of California, you can even learn someone's communication style by the way they move their eyes and words through neurolinguistic programming (NLP). If we know someone's communication style and know how they make decisions in that style, rapport and trust will come much faster. When you gain trust, you will always achieve a better deal. With trust, the other side will even rationalize why they want to do business with you.

Since listening is the most important thing you will ever do in a negotiation, you'd better become an expert at it. We will discuss advanced listening steps like the five-step bridge, the seven steps to becoming a great listener, and how to use the "let's assume" technique to find out the bottom line of what the other side wants.

Nonverbal communication is critical in any negotiation. Your negotiation partner will show you their thoughts long before they say it. You will also learn about how to gain trust by proximity in where you sit or stand. We will discuss the five things to look out for when people accept a deal, and how you can talk yourself out of a negotiation by not recognizing these five buying signals.

It's not enough to recognize when people accept the deal. You must also know the signals they use to show you when they disagree or are stressed. Whether you are face-to-face, on a video call, or on only a voice connection, you need to be able to read emotions in any situation.

Have you ever received a complaint? Has the customer or client ever been emotional? What is your process of dealing with these people? Do you have a system? Dealing with complaints is all about deescalation and negotiation. You never want to leave a client or customer feeling cheated. But you also want to communicate with rational customers. So the question becomes, how do you both deescalate emotions and negotiate a reasonable deal with someone who is not rational to begin with?

Lastly, we will talk about the attributes of a great negotiator. How do they think? What is their mindset? What are their beliefs? How do they deal with irrational partners? Negotiation is not always about a calm, collected discussion between two reasonable and rational business people. Sometimes it is trying to do a deal with the seller who overvalues their product or service. They may also become annoyed when the buyer does not recognize how valuable that is.

In my book *Why Smart People Make Dumb Mistakes with Their Money*, I discuss the *endowment effect*. In one University of Chicago study, students were given coffee cups that had a suggested price of $5. Since the student received the cups for free, they could sell them for any price they wanted. But even with no cost of goods, the average sold price was $4.75. Presumably the students could have sold many more cups at a lower price. But the cups were their possession and therefore, in their minds, commanded a higher value. This is why it's so entertaining to see sellers negotiate prices for heirlooms at garage sales and pawnshops. The product has a lot more value to the seller than to the buyer.

This book will cover all parts of negotiation from basic gambits to advanced skills. It will also discuss the psychological makeup of constructing in creating a negotiation deal. If you read it cover to cover, you will never be on the losing side of any future negotiation. After reading this book, you will feel confident, knowing that you have the ability and skills to succeed in any negotiation you want.

If you want to maximize what you learn from this book, read one chapter every day. Apply what you learn within twenty-four hours, and tell one person about what you've discovered. Psychological studies have shown that within twenty-four hours, we forget 70 percent of what we read and hear. After three days, we forget 90 percent. If you don't apply these techniques within one day, you're less likely to have these skills available when you need them most.

The best negotiators have a mindset for getting a good deal. They enjoy learning about techniques, applying the skills, and using the skills with other people. *Mindset* here means always thinking about using negotiation tactics. There are many situations where applying these skills isn't worth your time, but there are many others where negotiating is as simple as asking for what you want.

The more you use these techniques, the more comfortable you will become. In the beginning, you will feel awkward using them, since you are so unpracticed. But like any skill, the more you utilize it, the more comfortable you will become. So start small.

Ask a server in a restaurant if there are any discounts on desserts. Are there two-for-one deals available for the products you want to buy? Before you redo your gym membership, ask the manager—*not* the desk clerk—if you can get two months free with your annual renewal.

One of my clients works with a personal trainer at a local gym. She is usually exhausted after a simple thirty-minute workout. But the training packages come in only one-hour segments. She could have just accepted what the gym offered and avoided the discomfort of negotiating for what she wanted. After only a couple of negotiation lessons, she offered to buy the five-session package, but only if they would split them into ten. The manager at first said they only offered sixty-minute sessions. But when my client graciously said no and started to walk out the door, the manager relented and decided to make an exception.

This is an example of simply applying negotiation techniques. All my client did was ask for something she wanted, and she was prepared to walk out if she didn't get it. There was no downside, since she could have easily walked back in the fitness center and accepted the standard package.

This is how effective negotiation techniques will be for you. All you have to do is try. Start small, develop confidence in your ability, and then grow your requests into increasingly bigger deals.

Please read this book and let me know what you think. Contact me at:

www.KerryJohnson.com

Kerry@KerryJohnson.com; 714-368-3650

Twitter, @DrKerryJohnson;

LinkedIn, Kerry Johnson, MBA, PhD

1

Negotiation Strategies and Skills

Every negotiation is based on tools you can use appropriately. These skills will help you whether you are negotiating a used car deal, your kids' bedtime schedule, or your next salary increase. Hundreds of negotiation gambits are available, but the ones I'm listing below are the thirteen most useful techniques you can use.

As I stressed in the introduction, it's critical that you apply each of these techniques within twenty-four hours of learning them.

Rarely will you have the time to check your notes before delivering a response. All these skills should be memorized and pulled from your quiver when needed. Many of my clients will list these strategies on three-by-five cards and review these notes before every major negotiation.

Here are the thirteen strategies and skills you will use most often.

Strategy 1: Never Jump at the First Offer

The first technique we are going to talk about is, *never jump at the first offer.* Do you remember the last time you sold a car? Have you ever sold anything at a garage sale? Did you get the best price possible? How did you know? Let's assume a buyer wanted to make an offer for your used 1956 Chevy. It's a classic, and you have loved it for thirty years, but now it's time to sell. You really want $35,000. The buyer wants to pay $25,000, and you say OK. But a day after the deal, you have buyer's remorse. You might have done better. You will never know, because you jumped at the first offer.

Let's look at the situation from the other side. Suppose you offered $25,000 for a $35,000 Chevy. The seller immediately accepted it. Do you think you got a good deal? No, you probably thought there was something wrong with the car; otherwise they would not have said yes so quickly. So, you see, negotiation not only produces a good price but also creates confidence in the buyer and the seller that both got a good deal.

The other reason you should never say yes to the first offer is buyer's remorse. In the Chevy example, your offer of $25,000 for the $35,000 car is immediately accepted. What is your first thought? What a great deal I got? I can't believe how lucky I am? No. You would probably think you could have gotten a better deal.

But there's also another side to this story. If the seller won't negotiate at all, it might create annoyance and irritation. In a way, you can think of negotiation as the only fair way of reaching a deal. If someone simply walks away from your asking price without negotiating, you may feel rejected. On the other hand, if you engage and can't reach agreement, you both will know why and are unlikely to have hard feelings.

I bought my first house, in Irvine, California, for $256,000. (The joke is that in California, you can still buy a $300,000 house for $1.5 million.) But the seller wouldn't negotiate. I was at a disadvantage, since my Realtor walked the neighborhood asking homeowners to sell. This owner would only sell on the condition that they got full asking price. I was so irritated that they wouldn't engage that I threatened to walk away unless they threw in their new IBM personal computer. At least I got something, no matter how trivial. Just engaging in a negotiation makes both sides feel better.

You have worked for the same company for three years for the same low income. You are ready for a raise. You think any increase would be good. After all, a raise is really an indication of how much the company appreciates your work. The problem is, your boss has said no to your requests multiple times in the past. Is there really any point in asking again? After succeeding on a particularly tough project, you muster the courage. You walk in the office and once again ask for a raise. This time the boss agrees to a 5 percent increase. You are overjoyed, and, in the heat of the battle, you agree with gratitude. But was the boss willing to give you a 10 or even 20 percent increase? Would he have given you more vacation time off? Would he have included a car lease in the package? You will never know.

Why? Because you accepted the first offer. Often when we feel awkward and anxious about asking, we tend to accept any offer to release the anxiety of the negotiation. Your request does not have to be contentious. You can appeal for a raise by citing past successes and performance.

This is the way you need to approach any negotiation: You want a better deal. They offer something that seems reasonable. But you need to be confident for yourself that you deserve the best deal without burning any bridges in the process. This can be done with respect, humor, and even humility. In fact, these attributes will help you get the deal you want.

We will discuss the psychological makeup of a great negotiator later in the book. But look at any negotiation as one that will achieve a great deal for both you and the other party. Be confident that you deserve the best deal you can get.

My wife, Merita, is an American Airlines flight attendant. She and I can fly for free. This is called *nonrevenue* or *nonrev*. Although I pay for all my airline tickets to and from speaking events, leisure travel is a different story. All airline employees are fairly experienced travelers. We all know how to book a flight and check in twenty-four hours ahead of the departure. Most savvy nonrev flyers will check in with the departure gate agent and let them know we are here. But surprisingly, the gate agents will announce the name of the passenger and hand out a boarding pass without asking if the seat is acceptable. Most nonrevs are grateful to have a seat, or don't know how to negotiate. I fly nearly 8,000 miles a week and know the configuration of nearly every airplane American flies. My favorite seats are the exit rows in coach, since there is more legroom. Generally, when I'm handed a boarding pass, I ask for an exit row seat. Then the negotiation starts. If there are no exit rows, I will ask whether any bulkhead or exit row passengers have yet to check in. I will even ask if any rows are empty. This is especially helpful on an international flight so that you can lie down and sleep.

You need to be able to ask. You need to risk rejection. You need to be able to deal with no. I have even been able to negotiate my way into a first-class seat, although rarely. On one flight from Shanghai, China, I was facing a fourteen-hour nonrev in a no legroom economy seat. I noticed that one of the first-class seats was not occupied. I asked the gate agent why and she said the seat was broken and couldn't put any revenue passengers in it. I then reminded her that I was a nonrev and wouldn't mind sitting in a broken first-class seat. Actually, the only problem with the seat was that it would not fully recline, but it was certainly better than a coach seat. I was able to get the deal I wanted to sit in first class. The gate agent was able to open up another seat on the airplane to accommodate one more passenger. It was truly a win-win negotiation.

KEY TAKEAWAYS

1. Don't say yes to the first offer or counteroffer. You will be left feeling, "I could have done better," or, "Something must be wrong."

2. Create a negotiation mindset. Think about negotiating in any appropriate interaction. Whether it is business, family, or even organizing an event, think about how you can negotiate something better.

3. As you avoid saying yes to the first offer, be prepared for the other side's better offer. Always have the end in mind during a

negotiation. But always realize there is more room to negotiate until the other side walks away.

Strategy 2: Negotiation Isn't Only about Price

Negotiations are not always about money. Often it is about delivery speed, quality of the product or service, financing terms, warranty, follow-through, access to other services within a company, peace of mind, and reliability.

In fact, most high-level negotiations are only partly about price. They are more frequently about the whole package. In his book *Selling to VITO the Very Important Top Officer*, my friend Anthony Parinello discusses one negotiation at the University of California at San Diego (my alma mater). Tony responded to a request for proposal (RFP). He knew that all of his competitors would sell at a loss if it meant getting the business. Tony asked the provost if he was more concerned with price or cost, explaining that price is what you pay right now; cost is what you pay over the long run. The provost realized that service, follow-up, reliability, and company stability were more important than the immediate price. Tony was able to move from having to compete with those selling at a loss to negotiating a deal for a whole package of services.

Which nonprice benefits are you willing to give up? Would you give up reliability? Would you give up follow-up service in case your purchase has issues? Would you give up delivery because the price was attractive? I recently negotiated on eBay for a new Wilson Clash tennis racket. The seller wanted $180. I offered $140.

The seller accepted $150. But would I have negotiated at all if there were no chance of returns, or if delivery would have taken months? I had the PayPal guarantee to fall back on in case of fraud. Even when you're buying a tennis racket, there are many factors to consider besides the price.

Think of the negotiations you've had in the past. Were they only about price? Were there assumptions about service, delivery, and warranties that made you feel comfortable enough to negotiate price in the end?

HOW GEORGE LUCAS BECAME A BILLIONAIRE

One of the most lucrative negotiations in history was conducted by one of the most unlikely negotiators. George Lucas, of *Star Wars* fame, was about to negotiate a deal that would eventually create billions of dollars in personal wealth—all because he realized that other aspects of a negotiation could create a lot more value than just price.

In 1974, George Lucas had recently finished producing and directing *American Graffiti*, a very popular movie. But when Lucas approached 20th Century Fox with his next project, the offer was insufficient. Fox wouldn't budge from paying Lucas $100,000 for directing and an additional $100,000 for producing the original *Star Wars*. But George Lucas had an idea. He wanted the merchandising rights to all the Star Wars characters. Like Walt Disney, he understood that merchandising from theme parks, dolls, keepsakes, and toys were more valuable than box office sales.

In 1977, *Star Wars* became an instant hit, and Lucas quickly became a millionaire. But his billionaire status was due to his negotiation skill. Today he is worth $5.3 billion, mostly from the sale of Lucas Films, his production company to Disney, which has produced additional series and extension movies based on the original Star Wars concept. Practically everyone on the face of the earth has seen a Star Wars brand product or film. Lucas would probably have been paid more money for the second installment of Star Wars. But if he had only negotiated fees and price, he may not have become a billionaire. Because of his creativity in negotiating for things other than price, Lucas struck gold.

When my friend sold his tree service for $30 million, he took some of the profit and created a mobile repair company servicing train locomotives. For railroad companies, the expense of repairing a locomotive is enormous. They have to take it out of service, transport it to a repair yard, then deliver the repaired locomotive back to the line. A repair service that makes house calls could save the company enormous amounts of money.

Yet when my friend tried to sell his service, he hit a brick wall. Engineers would be out of a job. Maintenance workers would be displaced. All of his would cause union issues, strikes, and downtime. My friend lost $2 million in the first year and hoped to break even by the second year. Price isn't everything. Sometimes price is the least important thing.

Many vendors are very willing to negotiate nonprice issues. For example, if you agree to pay the sticker price but asked for overnight shipping, you may encounter less resistance. What if you considered buying a mattress but wanted a quicker delivery time than the company was offering? You could agree to the price but ask the vendor to deliver it within a week. The vendor is likely to say, "I'll do the best I can." But with your superior negotiation skills, you would reply with, "I really want to buy the mattress, but only if you will guarantee delivery within seven days." It might be a lot easier for them to accept your offer instead of a 25 percent discount in price.

Hotel rooms are notoriously easy to negotiate, especially if you have status. Perhaps Hilton lists a price of $150 per night for a room. You ask to speak to the manager and explain that you would love to stay three nights if they will upgrade to a suite. The manager wants to fill rooms and realizes that empty ones don't make money. He's likely to agree (although he might ask you not to tell anybody about the deal). The difference in price between the $250 suite and the $150 standard room is $100. By negotiating something other than price, you actually made money.

The top-rated CNBC program *Shark Tank* has a goal of funding entrepreneurs with innovative products and services. The capital comes from panelists including Kevin O'Leary, Mark Cuban, and Barbara Corcoran. Often the sharks will make a low-priced offer for the majority of ownership in the new venture. Every episode ends up as a negotiation between the sharks and the entrepreneurs. When the price reaches an impasse, the shark is likely to sell their experience in helping startups succeed. Once in a while, the entrepreneur will accept a lower price offer because it enables them to work with a well-known shark, who could help them grow faster than they could on their own.

Another CNBC standout is *The Profit*. It stars Marcus Lemonis as a venture capitalist trying to save struggling companies. Lemonis' favorite sentence is, "When I have skin in the game, any company I work with will become successful, as long as they do what I tell them to." In every episode, he either walks away from a lost cause or makes an offer based on the current value of the company. He gives the founder between 8 and 49 percent of the value; then he always takes over the top management position, sometimes even going so far as to fire the founder and owner. In every episode, he emphasizes that the money he puts up is only a small part of the investment. His expertise, time, and knowledge are much more important than the capital he invests.

From these examples, you can see that money is not necessarily the most important aspect of a negotiation. There are many other factors that could be as or more important than the cash.

KEY TAKEAWAYS

1. Listen for areas besides money that are important to the other side.
2. Ask the other side how important those concerns are.
3. Work those concerns in when appropriate.

Strategy 3: Be Prepared to Deal with No

You need to take the chance of being rejected. A hotel manager may not be motivated to give you a deal if the property is at full occupancy. But at least you asked. At least you attempted to negotiate.

Former president Donald Trump brags about the money he makes negotiating hotels and New York City office buildings worth hundreds of millions of dollars. But he doesn't mention that he walks away from 10 times more deals than he accepts.

Trump succeeded at stopping unfair Chinese business practices during his presidency. At one point, the US and Chinese delegations reach an agreement to buy more US goods. At the last minute, the Chinese changed the deal. The only thing that saved the negotiation was that the Trump told the American delegation to walk away, installing major tariffs on Chinese goods. When the Chinese realized they could not roll the administration, as they had in the past, they signed the agreement. You have to be able to walk away from a bad deal. But you also have to be willing to attempt to negotiate to get a good deal.

THE MAGICAL WORD *BECAUSE*

Often *how* you ask for an accommodation is as important as the ask itself. One Harvard research study showed that using the word *because* creates impressive compliance. In some instances, a student walked to the front of a line of students, who were waiting to make photocopies. She asked if she could cut in line. Only 13 percent of her attempts were successful. In other instances, she was instructed by researchers to use the word *because* in the request. She said, "Do you mind if I cut in line, *because* I have a deadline?" She was able to get 83 percent compliance using this word. One researcher wondered whether it was the result of how she asked or of the word alone. She then went to another photocopy line and used *because* without any other explanation: "Do you mind if I make some photocopies, *because* I need to make some photocopies?" This totally redundant request also achieved an 83 percent acceptance rate.

How you ask is as important as the negotiation itself. For example, you might say, "I would love to stay three nights at your hotel if you could upgrade me to a suite, *because* I have a very important meeting with clients who would love to see how gorgeous your property is." Or you might say, "I would love to spend three nights at your hotel, *because* I would love to recommend your property as a conference destination for my clients. Will that be OK?"

I'm sure you can see the difference between a mere request and the power of adding the word *because*. I will say more about the psychological aspects of negotiation later in this book. But try this today: make a request of somebody, and use the word *because*. Also notice whether you are able to gain more rapport, attention, or even a smile. It's a magical word that most people will respond to.

KEY TAKEAWAYS

1. Enter every negotiation prepared to hear no.
2. Enter every negotiation expecting the other side to desire a negotiated deal instead of no deal.
3. Use the word *because* whenever you make a request.

Strategy 4: Ask for More Than You Expect to Get

Have you ever thought you could have done better?

Would you ever ask for a raise bigger than what you want?

If you received a bad meal at an expensive restaurant, would you dare ask to cancel the entire bill, even though you know that it is unlikely?

Would you ask for a discount, knowing that the seller has a reputation for never offering deals?

Many years ago, I became irritated at the cost of electricity for my home in Southern California. The summertime bills charged by Southern California Edison were $600 per month. To get my bills below $25 a month, I was convinced solar power was the answer. The problem was installation. The cost was $45,000, with a $8,000 credit from the state of California. I thought of trading a speech, or at least audio and video training programs, to offset the expense. I had done that a few times before, bartering my products for outdoor furniture and even a barbecue, but these were trades of a few thousand dollars at most.

I found one company that had a great reputation: LA Solar. I called the owner and asked for a quote. I was tempted to ask for a discount, bartering for audio and video programs or even a training session. Instead, I asked to trade my services for the whole installation cost of $37,000. The owner agreed to the trade, but only if I coached his whole sales team as well as working on his management and recruiting skills. I was shocked. I never realized any company would agree to a trade for that much money. My theory had always been that companies would barter for their profit, not their cost of goods. This is why you should always ask for more than you expect to get: you just might get it.

There are many other benefits of asking for more. The other side may feel like they got a good deal too. Since you overstated your demands, you can always rationalize that you settled for less.

The biggest reason this strategy succeeds is people's natural inclination to compromise. It's rare for people to take a hard line. They will almost always give up something.

The most frequent negotiations we do are with our own family. You ask a child to clean up their room. They ask to postpone the chore until after dinner. Your spouse wants to take the nice car to see some friends, but you also want to drive it at that time. You compromise by letting her take the car if she agrees to have it back by a certain time so that you can use it too.

I have adapted to the superior negotiation skills of my youngest daughter, Caroline. Recently I asked her to clean up her dishes on the stove. She said she would only agree after I did my own dishes. She negotiates without even knowing it. These days I'm learning to ask for more than I expect to get. If I want her to clean, I first ask if she will do the whole kitchen. When she balks, I ask if she will at least clean up her dishes. This usually works.

One of the best negotiators in US political history is Henry Kissinger. He opened the US to mainland China and extracted America from the Vietnam War. At an advanced age, Kissinger is still a brilliant negotiator, doing deals around the world. He once said, "Effectiveness at the conference table depends upon overstating one's demands." One of his favorite tactics is to always ask for more than he expects to get.

During the 2015 Iran nuclear negotiations, the US government wanted a full disarmament of Iranian nuclear weapons. Iran wanted all of its assets repatriated that had been frozen during the Iranian hostage crisis, dating back to Jimmy Carter's presidency. The assets amounted to more than $150 billion. Not only did the Iranian government get all the money they requested, but they also got a short pause of 10 years on weapons development. As a bonus, they were paid hundreds of millions of dollars to release

American hostages. They asked for more than expected to get, and got it all I am sure they thought they could have done better.

The Trump administration pulled America out of the nuclear weapons agreement, putting severe economic sanctions on the Iranian government. As of this writing, the Iranians are at the negotiation table again, asking for more than expect to get. They are demanding that all sanctions be dropped as well as asking for another short pause in nuclear weapons development. Let's see if their strategy works once again.

In the early 1990s, President George H.W. Bush faced an invasion of Kuwait by an aggressive Saddam Hussein of Iraq. The American administration made drastic demands of Iraq. First was to leave Kuwait. Second, Saddam was to restore the legitimate government of Kuwait and make monetary reparations for the damage inflicted on Kuwait. Hussein would also have to allow inspections of all military personnel and hardware.

There was no way Saddam Hussein could have agreed to all this. His authoritarian grip on power hinged on fear. Agreeing to all these demands would have weakened his rule and triggered his overthrow. The American government knew this, but never intended to negotiate. They wanted to defeat the Iraqi military. They didn't want its 600,000 soldiers on the Kuwaiti border, waiting to invade later. Either outcome was good: Saddam would have been either deposed or militarily defeated. President Bush asked for more than he expected to get. He was unwilling to settle for anything less.

When Iraq was defeated by a coalition of ten countries, it retreated to its own borders. But soon Saddam tried to assassinate

President Bush on a trip to the Middle East and continued to create instability. In 2003, George W. Bush, the forty-third president, again made a demand of Saddam Hussein. Again, it was more than Bush 43 expected to get and more than Saddam could give. Bush wanted Saddam to give up all his weapons and leave Iraq. Like his father, he knew that Saddam could never meet those demands. But Bush also wanted to invade Iraq, knowing it was the only way to take Saddam Hussein out and end any further threat.

Sometimes professional negotiators will tempt you to negotiate. A car dealership or a real estate developer entices you by promising that any offer will be considered. This is only a way to get you in the door. You will be tempted to ask for more than you expect to get. They will counter with something less, and you will likely compromise. This is what professional negotiators do. But unless you have the skills of a professional negotiator, you will not get what you want.

When you're facing a professional negotiator, it's probably better to let someone else represent you. This is partly why attorneys are able to make better deals than their clients. Clients are too emotionally involved, and they don't have the skills to negotiate effectively. The next time you are tempted to visit a dealership to buy your dream car, either read this book cover to cover, or take someone with you. Tell your partner the deal you want. Then give them permission to drag you off the car lot, forcibly if necessary, instead of agreeing to a bad deal. Don't become the victim of a better negotiator.

Of course, our children are brilliant at asking for more than they expect to get. My good friend, negotiation expert Roger

Dawson, told me of his son, Dwight, who at age sixteen wanted to borrow dad's new Corvette. Roger said no. Then Dwight said, "If you won't let me drive the Corvette, can I at least borrow the mini-van?" Roger agreed.

Thirty minutes later, three of Dwight's fellow band members came by with drums and equipment for a gig that night. Roger realized that Dwight never wanted the Corvette. But Dwight knew that he might not get the minivan by asking for it first. So why not ask for the Corvette and settle for the minivan, which he wanted all along? Instinctively Dwight knew how to ask for more and make his dad compromise down to what he really wanted.

KEY TAKEAWAYS

1. Ask for more, because you just may get it.
2. Asking for more than you expect to get, but then letting the other side compromise, allows you both to win.
3. Ask for more than you expect to get, because people naturally tend to split the difference.

REJECTION, THEN RETREAT

Asking for more than you expect to get is based on getting something, if not everything. If you own a clothing store and want to sell an expensive suit plus a tie and dress shirts, would you start with the cheapest item, the tie, and upsell? Or would you sell the most expensive item, the suit, and add products on your way down?

Common sense states that you would start small and upsell. But using the principle of asking for more than you expect to get, you would sell everything at once and be prepared to settle for something less. For example, you would show the customer some suits to find one he likes. Then you would show the same customer various shirts. Lastly, you show the customer a few ties to determine which matched the suit and shirts.

At the very end of the closing presentation, you would ask if the customer wanted to buy all the items. If yes, you got lucky. You never thought they would agree to everything. But what if they agreed to buy only the suit and shirts? This is still more than you thought you would sell.

One of my coaching clients presented a retirement plan to a sixty-five-year-old man. The investable assets were nearly $1 million. My client requested that he put $400,000 in the stock market and another $600,000 into safe investments like annuities. The client initially said no. He didn't want to allocate all his money to the same financial advisor. But my client remembered the concept of rejection, then retreat. He said, "Would you at least like to put $400,000 of your assets into safe money to protect it from volatility?" The client agreed, and my coaching client made a sale. It wasn't the whole $1 million, but it was at least part. My client kept in contact with the retiree and later on was able to gain the rest.

We have a very strong inclination to reach a compromise when offered. It's only when there's an either/or decision that we may decide no.

KEY TAKEAWAYS

1. When getting a no, back off to a lesser concession.
2. A no doesn't mean rejection. It means that particular concession is unacceptable.

Strategy 5: Bracketing

Have you ever bought or sold something and wondered if you got a good price? It's amazing: whether I'm selling a car, computer, or sports equipment, the price ends up being midway between the asking and offer price. One of my first cars was a Sunbeam Alpine, a British convertible. The Sunbeam Tiger had a huge engine and was a collector's item, but the Alpine, while nice, wasn't worth nearly as much. In 1971, I advertised it for $7,000. A buyer offered $6,000. Can you predict what we settled on? You got it: $6,500.

We've discussed the human tendency towards compromise. We want to reach common agreement, no matter how vast the differences. When my wife and I are far apart on an issue, we will almost always try to reach common ground. Recently I called a friend to play tennis at 8:30 a.m. He didn't want to play until 10:00. Guess what time we started? 9:15. In any negotiation, each side tends toward reaching the middle. This is what makes bracketing work so well.

Bracketing is a method of reaching a compromise of your choosing, instead of where the negotiation ends up. Since the final price is always in the middle, you should set your price predicting where the middle will be. Never make the first offer. You will always be bracketed. If the sticker on a used car is $20,000, and you want to pay $18,000, offer $16,000. If the seller wants $500 for a Trek bike, and you want to buy it for $400, offer $300. You get the point. You need to set your offer predicting where the middle will end up.

Recently I bought a pair of Babolat shoes from a tennis shop. The owner, James, is a nice guy and always gives me a discount. But this time, James was gone, and his son was in the shop. I asked, "How much for the shoes?"

He said, "$120."

"James always gives me a discount, but I forgot how much it is. Would you take $99 for the shoes?"

"How about $110, including tax?"

I smiled and said, "Sounds good. Thanks." Bracketing always works.

Think of the myriad ways you can use bracketing. If the seller wants to charge a $5 shipping fee for a package to arrive in seven days, you can bracket by asking for overnight delivery without cost. The seller may laugh or even tell you that he is losing money, but I guarantee the final compromise will be in the middle.

What if you need to cancel an order for tables and chairs? The cancellation fee is 50 percent, but things have changed and you need to reschedule for six months later. The event company wants their 50 percent of the deposit. You want all the money back with the promise that you will reschedule soon. Guess where the negotiation ends up? Probably with 25 percent deposit and a new contract for the next event.

Sometimes bracketing can go substantially in your favor without a compromise. I bought an HP printer recently. It arrived damaged. The repair shop owner gave it a once-over and said it was unrepairable. I called the seller and asked for my money back. I was on solid ground, since I had received a damaged product. The seller offered to refund the money and apply it towards another, better printer at no extra cost. She even offered to pay the shipping. I countered by saying I needed the printer in three days and asking if she would include the color toner cartridges as well. She agreed to everything without asking for any more concessions. A real middle-of-the-road bracket would have been to get a refund, but only if I shipped the damaged printer back at my expense. You will usually get what you want if you use these skills.

President Bill Clinton was impeached by Congress in the 1990s. Do you remember how it all started? Paula Jones accused then Governor Clinton of sexual harassment. She sued him for $1 million. During his presidency, Clinton offered Jones $500,000. Guess how much the final settlement was after the presidency? $750,000.

The irony is, if Clinton had settled with Jones out of court using a nondisclosure agreement, he would not have been accused of lying in a deposition, lost his Arkansas law license, or have been impeached. Just one negotiation could have saved Clinton a great deal of grief and embarrassment. His defense legal fees alone were more than the settlement cost. The greater irony was that Bill Clinton was actually a very good negotiator. The problem was, he didn't use his superior negotiation skills personally. He left it to his lawyers. Arguably he was poorly served by those who represented him.

Here is an example of how good Bill Clinton's negotiation skills were. In 1993, Mexico was on the verge of financial default. They wanted an $82 billion loan from the United States. But Mexican president José López Portillo balked at the $100 million fee the US was charging to broker the loan. Although Portillo balked at the brokerage fees, ended up paying $50 million. This is another good example of bracketing.

The trick to bracketing is getting the other side to make the first offer. If you state your position first, the other person can bracket you. The art is in how you ask. For example, if a seller states a car is $20,000 and you bracket at $16,000, there's a chance the seller might say no and refuse to negotiate further. But since you are now becoming a master negotiator, you will use the word *because*. For example, "Your car is beautiful and certainly worth $20,000. But I need a dependable car for my daughter, *because* I am worried about any car breaking down and stranding her in the middle of the night. It's way too dangerous for a young college student. Would you consider $16,000 to help out my daughter?" Of course, the final amount will be $18,000.

Normally, communicating your needs and worries is irrelevant in a negotiation. But we are not negotiating robots. We have emotions and rationalize decisions. If the seller knows how badly you need a dependable car, they may respond more readily if you give them a reason—and of course use the magical word *because*.

Many years ago, after speaking in a seminar, I did my standard sales offer for audio-video educational materials. The price sheets were in the handouts I provided. While I was signing books, one middle-aged woman said she couldn't afford my programs but was desperate to use them. She was a single mom of three kids and had big expenses. She was sure that my educational materials would help her get to the next level of income. She asked if I would give her a discount because of her extraordinary needs. I asked how much of a discount she wanted. She said 50 percent on all the materials I offered.

I was the middle signing books and didn't want to dilute the sales of potential buyers around the product table. I asked if she would come back in fifteen minutes so we could talk. After the flurry of attendees buying books, audio programs, and videos, she reappeared. I sold her all the programs she wanted at 50 percent off, without bracketing. My reasoning was that she was sincere and would apply the techniques to help her family. I also rationalized that I didn't want to ship the materials back to my office. This is a very good example not only of the benefits of bracketing, but also of why and how you ask for a concession is as important as the concession itself.

KEY TAKEAWAYS

1. Decide on the price you want before the negotiation.
2. Bracket your counteroffer so that the middle becomes the price you want.
3. Always assume that people will split the difference.

Strategy 6: Flinching

Great negotiators will always flinch at proposals and offers. This means they will react with shock and surprise. When someone makes an offer, they will watch your reaction. Since most people are poor negotiators, they may not know how to get a better deal. Even if you don't make a counteroffer, the seller could add on extra expenses and fees unless you flinch.

I've made this mistake many times: I'm so excited to get the product or service that I accept the offer enthusiastically. Then I hear about all the extras. One website designer told me that a new template would only cost $500. I was expecting $1,000 and said that seemed fair. Then an extra $100 per month maintenance fee was added on—all because I didn't flinch at the initial $500 cost.

As I've mentioned, in 1989, my future wife, Merita, and I traveled to Berlin. During that trip, Merita saw a fur coat in the window of a high-end clothing store. The clerk said it cost $1,000. Trying to impress my girlfriend, I smiled, saying I expected it to be more. Beneath the smile, I was stressed, thinking I could barely afford it. But since I appeared happy to accept the offer, the clerk also mentioned there was a 23 percent state tax and a 5 percent boxing fee in addition to the price. If I have known about flinching, I could have saved $280 or more on that purchase, and possibly gotten a discount.

HOW TO FLINCH

Contrast that to another situation—perhaps buying artwork. The seller wants $100 for the piece. You flinch and say, "That seems like a lot of money." The dealer then offers to throw in a $25 frame and ship it free. You've gotten a $35 discount because you flinched. You don't want to appear rude. You would rather be polite and pleasant. But it doesn't pay to politely accept a price on which you can do better.

I heard one negotiation expert suggest practicing flinching in a mirror. You can scowl, roll your eyes, or even shake your head. The caveat is to only flinch when talking to an owner or manager. An hourly worker won't care a twit about your flinch. They don't have the power to give you a better deal. They don't care if you throw a tantrum or pound your fists on the ground.

Professional negotiators are elegant. Some experts recommend flinching to show the seller how outraged you are. They also recommend disparaging the product or service, saying it's not worth the price. But negotiation is all about engagement and relationship. If someone wanted to buy your services and told you how overpriced or lacking they are, would you be as willing to make price concessions? Or would you become defensive?

Many years ago, an investment real estate company wanted me to speak to their clients across the US. Their goal was to get funding and develop strip malls. They also realized more attendees would come to hear me speak than to hear a sales pitch from their wholesalers. The president of the company was a woman I called the "Velvet Hammer." She would build you up while getting all the concessions she wanted. At that time, my speaking fee was $5,000 per presentation. She wanted me to speak twenty times that year. She said, "You are absolutely the best speaker we've ever had. It's a joy to listen to you and see how you are able to light up an audience. You also are able to work our company services into your examples. The attendees are able to learn how to sell us to their clients. But your speaking fee is just too high. There's no way we can afford that kind of expenditure. It would be a shame if we couldn't use you to speak. But you're out of our price range. Is there way you can help us with your speaking fee?" With that, the Velvet Hammer would often get the deal she wanted. It was a sledgehammer with a sugar and honey coating.

Flinching can be mixture of nonverbal and verbal cues. It could be looking shocked and raising your voice as you say, "What?" It can be shaking your head while saying, "I had no idea it would be that expensive." Or it could be simply a harrumph while shaking your head. All of these flinches can work. Just make sure that you combine them with an elegant explanation.

Recently I returned from Lisbon, connecting through Dallas on American Airlines. I cleared customs much faster than I thought and tried to get an earlier flight to Los Angeles. But the ticket agent mistakenly erased my first-class seat and put me in a middle seat in the back of the airplane. I told this to a gate agent, who said there was nothing she could do. I stayed positive and asked for her supervisor. After fifteen minutes, he eventually showed up. He offered to put me in a first-class seat on a flight four hours later. I flinched by shaking my head and looking at the ground. I said, "I'm an Executive Platinum, your highest-level flyer. I love American Airlines. You all are the best folks in the airline industry. Do I really have to wait four hours just to get my seat back? Because of a mistake the ticket agent made? Do you think that's fair?"

The supervisor went back to his computer and upgraded me on my original flight, ahead of other passengers with more status. It might be tempting to think the supervisor wanted to correct a mistake, but it wasn't until I flinched that I got a better deal. Negotiation is not just about getting a better price. Negotiation is something that you can do every day to make you and your family's life better.

One important note in flinching is to be respectful. Today there's a lot of outrageous behavior. Vendors and providers may automatically push back. If you get upset, you may elicit entrenchment of their position. Especially when negotiating with airline employees, I always show empathy before I make a request. For example, in Madrid recently, I asked a gate agent for a better seat. First class was full, and I wasn't able to get an upgrade. But the flight was ten hours from Dallas.

I first said to the gate agent, "I know you are really busy and stressed as you close out this flight. But is there any way I could get a row to myself in coach?"

She said, "There are twenty on the standby list, and we will need all the seats."

I already knew there were ninety-five open seats on the flight. I said, "I really love to fly AA and have been an Executive Platinum for thirty years. You all have been so good to me all these years. Can you take another look and see if there are any rows that are open right now?"

You may be thinking this isn't really a negotiation, just a request. But my mention of thirty years of flying American Airlines implicitly suggests both continued loyalty and a veiled threat that I could fly the competition if she wasn't cooperative. Of course it worked. She even thanked me for my years of being an Executive Platinum.

Try to be a velvet hammer instead of an outraged, wronged traveler. The velvet hammer preserves relationships. The outraged traveler creates animosity. Even if you can get the deal you want. There may be some *rejection, then retreat* options available. For example, you may not be able to get a first-class seat on the flight leaving in one hour, but you may score a first-class seat on the next flight in three hours. Good-natured flinching is showing surprise and bewilderment. It is never attacking the other side.

Last week I wanted to play tennis with a friend, but all the courts were booked that day. Michael, the court director, offered the next day instead. I didn't really care, but I wanted to try out flinching. I said over the telephone, "Oh, my gosh. I really wanted to play today. That's crazy, it's so crowded. You are doing such a great job with the courts. Thanks for taking a look. But is there any way I can play today? There's nothing you can do to free up a court at 3:30?"

He said, "Let me look again. Maybe I can move one group to four o'clock and give you center court."

I thanked him profusely. Flinching is not being a jerk. Flinching is not being narcissistic or selfish. It's simply being direct with what you want while accepting the results. But it is a good tool to have when it really matters.

KEY TAKEAWAYS

1. Flinching may lead the other side to give you concessions.
2. Not flinching may lead the other side to add on extras.
3. Always be polite and respectful as you flinch.

Strategy 7: Never Offer to Split the Difference

One surefire sign of an amateur negotiator is offering to split the difference. It seems like the fair thing to do. After all, it's equally close to your offer and the asking price. Why not save time and propose a fair, middle ground solution?

You should never offer to split the difference, because the middle ground is never actually down the middle. If you offer to split the difference, the other side can agree and then split it again later. This could go on until it becomes a very bad deal. You attempt to be fair, but splitting the difference may become counterproductive.

You're at a flea market and want to buy a table. The seller wants $200, and you want to pay $150. You feel the simplest thing to do is to split the difference, getting to $175. This seems reasonable, doesn't it? It's really not worth haggling over $25. But then the seller goes to his wife and says, "The table is $200, and this guy wants to pay $150."

She says, "Go ahead and offer $190." He goes back to you with the new sales price. You then split the difference between $200 and $175, so the middle becomes $188.

The solution is never to offer to split the difference. If you offer $150 and they offer $200, just flinch or look disappointed. It always creates an offer to split the difference. If they make the offer, they are also more likely to stick with $175. They won't come back with another attempt to split.

The best way to motivate them to offer to split the difference is to say how much you want the deal while letting them know how frustrated you are. For example, you might say, "We are so close. I'm really frustrated that we can't make this happen. We have worked so long together. It is really frustrating. I don't know what to do."

There are very few people who won't step in to say, "Let's just split the difference." Then two things are likely to happen.

1. Since they offered to split the difference, they are also likely to stick with it.
2. You can then say that you will check with a higher authority and get back to them. This will allow you to present another offer and again split the difference. Depending on how much you want a better deal, this can be used to find out the other side's bottom line.

The most obvious benefit of this tactic is to prevent the other side from continually splitting the difference. Another benefit is to make the other side think they won the negotiation because they made the offer. Negotiation, as we've discussed before, is not a win-lose, zero-sum game. It's developing a relationship, setting the stage for future negotiations. It's making the other side feel good about the outcome.

Many years ago, a group offered to pay me $5,000 to speak. I wanted $7,500 for the program. I made a big mistake by saying, "What do you say we just make it $6,250? Is that OK with you?"

The meeting planner said, "Wonderful. I just have to get an OK from the president."

She called the next day and said, "He thinks $6,250 is too much; would you take $5,500 for the program?"

I made two mistakes. The first was to make the offer. Second was not negotiating with the decision maker. I was trying to bargain with an administrative person who couldn't say yes.

I should have said, "We are $2,500 apart. I would love to do this presentation, especially since it fits all your goals. You want the attendees to increase their closing skills, get more referrals, and manage their time more effectively. We are so close to settling on speaking fee. What you think we should do?"

The meeting planner would either have offered to split the difference or said that she would talk to her boss and see what she could do. She would have come back the next day and said her boss wants to split the difference. If I agreed to the proposal, that would have been the end of the negotiation.

It's important for you to have a good fundamental knowledge of negotiation techniques, but you also need to be an amateur psychologist in predicting behavior in any negotiation. Master negotiators have years of experience and have made many mistakes. You don't have to make your own mistakes. You can learn from others. But you have to practice these skills whenever you get the opportunity.

KEY TAKEAWAYS
1. Most people will offer to split the difference.
2. Never offer to split the difference.
3. Splitting the difference could go on forever until the deal becomes unprofitable.

Strategy 8: The Vise

The vise technique is a way to get the other side to immediately produce their best offer. One very effective technique is to balk at a proposal. No matter how good the price, the delivery terms, or even the quality, ask for more. Put them in an emotional vise. One way to do this is to say, "You'll have to do better than that." Then be quiet. If you really want to get the best deal in any negotiation, you will make good eye contact and be silent. The next person to talk will make a concession. It cannot be you.

The difference between a flinch and a vise is all about nonverbal signals. The flinch is a scowl, a grimace, or shaking the head. The verbal flinch is saying, "Oh, no," or "Wow, I had no idea it was that expensive." The vise is much more direct.

An inexperienced negotiator will hear the vise and immediately give you a better offer. A master negotiator will say, "How much better do you want?" You will soon discover that a lot of negotiation is getting the other side to make not only the first offer but also their best offer. There is a theory in the retail business that a big discount is usually from an already inflated price to begin with. A microwave oven with a 50 percent discount at Costco may have been overpriced before the discount. This is why the vise so often gets results.

A friend heard me speak about negotiation techniques and decided to try this method out. He took a client and four colleagues to a five-star restaurant and ordered entrées. The meal was already going to cost well over $500 with drinks and food. The waiter asked if anybody wanted wine. My client saw his opportunity. He asked how much and what the waiter recommended. The waiter suggested five bottles at $150 each, totaling $750. My friend didn't want to ask for a cheaper wine in front of his client, so he applied his newfound vise technique. He said simply, "$750? You'll have to do better than that."

The waiter said, "How much better?"

My friend said, "A lot better."

"How about three bottles at $150, and I will comp the other two?"

My friend said, "That's a great deal; let's do it."

Once you use the vise, shut up. The next person to talk will make a concession. As a young author and speaker, I encountered many experienced and grizzled salespeople trying to tell me how to sell. I would often hear manipulative tactics like giving a pen to a prospect and saying, "What do you think?" Most salespeople cannot keep their mouths shut. They can't deal with silence. They usually oversell and step on their close. My favorite closing line is, "What are your thoughts?" and then wait for a response.

THE TAKEAWAY

If I hear a thirty-second pregnant pause, I will typically use the *takeaway*. The *takeaway* is simply an attempt to take the offer off the table, or suggest that the other side reject the offer: "If this is not right for you, I totally understand." If the prospect is interested, they will push back and say it works. If they aren't interested, that statement will bring them to a no more quickly.

You can use this same tactic with the vise. After saying, "You'll have to do better than that," wait for a response. Don't talk and step on your request. But if the pause from the other side is too long, do the takeaway. "If this isn't something you can do, we can go someplace else." If the other party wants to do business, the takeaway will produce a response.

Personally, I would not say, "You'll have to do better than that." I would soften it by saying, "That seems high, I come here a lot and enjoy this place so much, can you give us a better deal?" Instead of being demanding, I generally try to give the other side a compliment as a reason to negotiate.

I once heard the story of how the Secretary of State Henry Kissinger used the vise during the Vietnam war. He asked an undersecretary to produce a report on the political parties in Southeast Asia. After a week, the undersecretary finished a comprehensive report, presented in a leather-bound cover. Sec. Kissinger simply wrote, "You'll have to do better than that," and then send it back. The undersecretary reworked the report over the next week and resubmitted it. Again, Kissinger wrote, "You'll have to do better than that," and send it back again to be reworked. After three submissions, the undersecretary finally walked the latest report into Kissinger's office and said, "My team and I worked on this for two weeks. It is comprehensive. It is the best thinking and the best work my team and I have ever done." Kissinger then said, "In that case, I will read it." Kissinger knew how to get best efforts from his team. He was never willing to read a report unless it was the best work they could do.

You are using the vise to get the best deal the other side can offer. You really don't know what that deal is until you ask the question.

KEY TAKEAWAYS

1. Respond to a proposal by saying, "You'll have to do better than that."

2. If the vise is used against you, respond by saying, "How much better do I have to do?"

3. Don't end the negotiation until the potential outcome is less than what you can make per hour. Again, negotiation will yield the highest rate of pay that you will ever make.

Strategy 9: Good Cop, Bad Cop

Nearly every TV cop show displays a suspect in an interrogation room. The perpetrator is threatened by a detective who pounds his fists and curses. He promises to put the suspect in jail for the rest of his life. Then another detective later comes in the room smiling, handing out doughnuts and a cup of coffee. He says the first interrogator is crazy. He doesn't want the suspect to go to jail for the rest of his life. He really wants to help. Politely, the good cop asks for the truth so he can help the perpetrator get out of a jam. Scared, the suspect confesses everything. Behind the one-way mirror, the detectives smile and move on to the next case.

This is just TV fiction, isn't it? Actually, this has probably happened to you. You want a new car, but don't want to pay the sticker price. You suspect they will take 10 percent less, but the car is so popular that the dealership can't keep it in stock. The salesperson asks for the maximum price you will pay. He really wants to help, because he likes you so much. The sales manager (bad cop) asked the salesperson (good cop) how much he can get you up to. All of a sudden, you realize that the salesperson, who is not even on your side, is negotiating with the manager.

This happened recently when we were buying a house in the Algarve region of Portugal. Merita and I flew from Los Angeles to Lisbon. Then we drove three hours to the southwest corner of

Portugal to a beautiful fishing village turned tourist destination called Carvoeiro. When we were on vacation eighteen months earlier, we had seen this beautiful 2,000-square-foot house. The Realtor told us the sellers had just remodeled and raised the price by $50,000. When we arrived, we discovered the remodel was only two windowpanes.

I was irritated and offered $430,000 instead of the $480,000 the sellers wanted. The British Realtor said the sellers lived in Germany and were very difficult to work with. She said, "I will do my best because I like you so much. I would love to see you and your wife get this house. I can see how much you love the area." She called the sellers. Five minutes later, she asked if we would just pay the full price, because Germans are so difficult. This often happens when there's only one Realtor in a transaction, who is paid by the seller. The whole time, they act as if they're on your side. In reality they are only trying to maximize their own gain.

We also discussed a version of this in the section on splitting the difference. For example, the seller wants $100. You want to pay $80. You offer to split the difference and make it $90. The seller says they have to check with partner or spouse. They contact you the next day and say the partner is very difficult to work with. They tried as hard as they could, but the partner would not budge; can you just pay $100 and make their life easier? They worked very hard to convince the partner. As in the above example, the seller (good cop) is representing you to their partner (bad cop). But they aren't even on your side.

The good cop, bad cop scenario plays out in many ways. After church, Merita and I often go to a brunch spot in Charleston, South

Carolina. I am a vegan pescatarian. I don't eat meat, dairy, or chicken and try to stay away from processed foods. (I am a prostate cancer survivor and am always careful about cancer recurrence.) One week we went, only dairy, chicken, and beef combinations were on the menu, except for a shrimp roll. While it's excellent, I'd had the same meal three weeks in a row. I asked the server if they had any fish choices that were not on the menu. She checked in the kitchen and said, "I did my best. I really pleaded your case to get fish. But the kitchen isn't ready yet. It will have more choices later on this evening."

While this doesn't seem like a negotiation, the server was trying to preserve her tip by acting as if she was doing her best to convince the cook to make an exception. The conversation probably went like this: "Hey, Don. Do you want to make some fish right now? No? OK, I'll tell the customer." If I really wanted to push the issue, I would have asked to talk to the cook directly.

This is exactly what you need to do when faced with the bad cop scenario. Just ask to speak to the bad cop directly. When we discuss later how to deal with the higher authority, we will talk about how to identify the higher authority in the very beginning. But for now, never assume the good cop is on your side. If you do encounter the bad cop, don't communicate through the good cop. Insist on talking to the bad cop directly.

This gambit was used in the 1979 Iranian hostage crisis. President Jimmy Carter had been unsuccessful in getting the hostages out of Iran. Before Ronald Reagan took office, Carter's team told the Iranian government officials that Reagan was a cowboy. He would use the US military to decimate Tehran and murder all of the hostage takers. The Americans tried to convince the Iranian negotiators that Carter was the nice guy, but there was nothing he could do after Reagan became president.

In a twist, Reagan actually worked with the Carter administration, suggesting they would be much better off releasing the hostages before Reagan took office. The end result was a compromise. The hostages were released the day after Reagan took office. The Islamic terrorists feared what would happen if they kept the hostages any longer during Reagan's administration.

Be aware of the good cop, bad cop strategy. Unless someone has a financial incentive to help you, they are probably not on your side. I know this seems cynical, but even psychologists are often fooled by a good cop's charm.

KEY TAKEAWAYS
1. Identify the good cop, bad cop tactic.
2. Never allow the good cop to represent you to the bad cop.
3. When you discover the bad cop, ask to talk to them directly.

Strategy 10: Never Change Your Offer

When the other side uses the vise, a flinch, or even an offer to split the difference, don't respond by changing your offer. These are just gambits to readjust the negotiation starting point.

I've discussed my first attempt to buy a house in Portugal. I mentioned that the sellers, a German couple, were unwilling to negotiate, but I did not discuss my mistake in changing my initial offer.

The Realtor knew that we were leaving for Lisbon at 1 p.m. At 9:30 a.m., we made an offer for $430,000 instead of the asking price of $480,000. When the Realtor called and said the Germans wanted their full asking price, my wife said, "We are here anyway. Let's just increase our offer to $450,000."

Big mistake. If the Realtor and owners had been smarter, they would have bracketed the $450,000 and the $480,000 to $465,000. This would have been nearly the price they wanted. Fortunately for us, we were willing to walk away, mainly because the Germans were unwilling to engage.

Once you make an offer, never change it except in response to a counter offer or concession. Once you change your offer, a good negotiator will use it as the new starting point and create a bad deal for you.

There are many reasons for not countering your own offer. First, it lets the other side know that they can get whatever they want. If you cave so quickly without even demanding a counter-offer, you are communicating that you need the deal at any cost. You're also letting the other side know that you aren't credible. If you make an offer and change it without reason, the other side knows that you don't even have faith in what you offered.

One of my Realtor friends was able to get home buyers into a bidding war in the beginning of 2021, during the hottest market in thirty years. The sellers wanted $2.1 million for the house. One buyer, following bad advice from his inexperienced Realtor, offered $1.9 million. The offer was made only two days after the home was listed. The sellers thought if they kept the listing open longer by rejecting the $1.9 million, they could get more money. That is exactly what happened. The buyer, hearing this, immediately increased the offer to $2.2 million—$100,000 over listing price. The crazy thing was, there were no other bidders. The sellers knew the buyer was desperate. They asked for six months of renting the property back while they picked out a new home in another city. What could the buyer do? He had already lost credibility by changing his offer so fast.

The answer is to make an offer and stick to it. If the other side doesn't counter, simply let them know you understand and will look at other products. Salespeople, such as Realtors, sometimes manipulate this. They tell buyers not to insult the seller by making an offer that is too low; supposedly the seller will get angry if the offer isn't high enough.

Responding takes some elegance. Make the offer by telling the seller how much you love their home or product. Also say that you totally understand if they don't want to accept the offer, but you wanted to try. If there is some level of rapport, the seller will at least engage and drop the price somewhat. If they counter, you have something to work with.

KEY TAKEAWAYS

1. Never change your offer except in response to the other party's offer.
2. Changing your offer will decrease credibility.

Strategy 11: Nibbling

Have you ever concluded a negotiation thinking you made a good deal? You had an agreement, but at the last minute, the other party wanted something more.

You're a real estate investor and agree to a price on a property. You estimate that you can make about $50,000 on it by painting, landscaping, and putting in new carpets. But at the last minute, the sellers nibble you. They want their out-of-state moving costs of $7,000 included in the deal. Compared to a profit of $50,000, an extra $7,000 doesn't seem like that much. But you've just decreased your profit by 14 percent. Then you get nibbled again. Then perhaps again, until there is no profit left.

How do you stop this from happening?

The answer is to never make a concession after an agreement without getting one in return. Children are brilliant nibblers. You agree to something, but at the last minute, they want a little more. When my daughter Catherine was sixteen years old, she wanted to borrow my car. I eventually said yes only after I got concessions that she would be home at ten o'clock, not drink, and not allow anybody else in the car. She agreed to all that. But right before walking out, she asked if she could have $10. She nibbled me. In comparison to the intense negotiation about taking the car, $10 was a minor concession. I didn't even have to think about the answer.

Don't fall for this tactic. The nibble is tempting, because the heavy lifting of the negotiation has already been done. The nibble seems minor by comparison. But when does it stop? Only when the cost of asking for more at the end is too high.

Here is how to stop the other side from nibbling: always get a concession in return. The nibbling will soon stop. When they find out they can't get something for free, it will no longer be worth it to ask.

One mortgage company agreed to pay my speaking fee if I did one presentation at 9 a.m. and another at 5 p.m. This meant spending the whole day at the meeting for a half-day speaking price. I agreed to the deal. I thought I was doing the client a favor.

As soon as I agreed, the favor was forgotten. The meeting planner delayed returning the contract. Eventually she said her boss wanted me to throw in 100 copies of my latest book for free. It would have been very easy to accept this nibble, since I was trying to get the contract back, but the cost of the books made it a worse deal. What else would they nibble if I agreed? They had already disregarded my favor of staying the whole day.

I countered the nibble by saying I would bring books for all the attendees but only speak for one hour in the morning, canceling the speech in the afternoon. The planner said no, they wanted me to speak twice that day. This stopped the nibble. They realized that any request would be traded for something I wanted. It wasn't worth asking for anything else. She ended up buying the books for all her attendees anyway.

Ironically, at lunch that day, the planner told me her tactic of asking for things at the end was a strategy she always used and one that always worked. No one ever said no.

But the planner continued to nibble even after telling me about her manipulative tactics. She said they wouldn't be able to pay for car mileage from my home in Newport Beach to San Diego, although this was in our written agreement. I empathized with her but said I would have to cut my speech short, since I would have to use the expensive toll roads to get home. She again backed down. While it was irritating to think she was trying to negotiate unfairly, she admitted I was the only speaker who ever pushed back.

Don't fall for the nibble. The other side may keep nibbling until you say no. If you accept the nibble, any agreement becomes less profitable. Don't be hypnotized by momentum. (Momentum is when you are invested in the deal and want to work to get it done. It can be hard to stop.) Don't invest so much that you can't say no. Always get a concession in return. It will stop the nibble immediately.

KEY TAKEAWAYS
1. When being nibbled, ask for a concession in return.
2. Don't expect the other party to remember any favors you do.
3. Be polite and empathetic when you push back against the nibble.

Strategy 12: Setting Up Yes

Unfortunately, most people don't like to negotiate. They are unsure of their skills and aren't well practiced. But those who learn how to use these skills enjoy using them. They want to get participation.

They want to get the other side to do a deal—sometimes any deal. They want the other side to at least engage.

This becomes particularly difficult when a buyer wants to negotiate and the seller refuses, or when the negotiation is close to being done, but one side walks away because of a bruised ego. Think about past negotiations where you have reached a good deal but still walked away. Why? Because you thought the other side was dismissive or disrespectful or didn't listen.

Sometimes even a small concession at the right time can save a deal; even making a small gesture can make the other side feel better and get them to yes. This isn't true in a retail environment, where clerks are paid by the hour and don't care whether you buy or walk away. They aren't involved in the profit or loss of the store; they only care about their hourly pay and when they can clock out. But when the other party is invested in the negotiation, even the smallest concession can make a difference.

IT'S NOT THE SIZE OF THE DEAL; IT'S THE TIMING

Here are a couple of ideas that make the buyer feel better and save a deal without costing much. These ideas will set up a yes without losing the customer.

1. You are selling an expensive drone and offer to show the buyer how to use it.

2. You sell high-end printers and offer to sell the first reorder of toner at your cost.

3. You are an eBay seller and receive an offer below what you want. You counter with a fair price and also offer a sixty-day return instead of thirty days.

4. You are a business coach and receive an offer of half-price for the first month of coaching. You don't want to accept it but also don't want to lose the client. You make them feel better by countering with full price but giving them all your audio and video programs ($699 value) as a concession if they sign up now. (Actually, I have done this in my practice.)

5. In response to a low offer, counter with an extended warranty of three years for the price of two.

Also, congratulate the other party on their willingness to negotiate. Tell them how much you enjoy engaging and how good they are at it. Tell them how few people negotiate and what a great deal they got.

APPEAL TO THEIR EGO

Self-esteem and ego are major parts of any successful negotiation. Both sides want to feel good about the deal. Even a good outcome can be ruined if the other side acts as if they've won. I've mentioned that many golfers negotiate bets on the first tee. One player says they haven't played in a year. The other reports a handicap that is much higher than it actually is. While it's all in good fun, there is often one who brags about outwitting the others. After scoring a birdie on the first hole, he might say, "I guess I'm a better golfer than I let on." The other players either will never bet again or will make that next negotiation contentious.

Years ago, I bought a pair of "end of the season" powder skis from a shop in Alta, Utah. The shop owner wanted $500 for some demos. I offered $350, because they were in good shape. We settled on $400. He made a concession of giving me extra ski wax. The wax was at most $20. But the owner threw in a minor concession, setting me up for a yes in the end.

As I left, another sales clerk said I could have gotten the skis for 25 percent less if I had waited only one more week. I don't know if the clerk was trying to brag about getting one over on me, but it made me irritated that I'd only accepted the wax as a concession. Fortunately, I realized it was still a better deal than I had been able to find before.

Even if you don't want to negotiate, offer something as an accommodation. It doesn't matter how small or how large. We want buyers to negotiate. We want them to walk away happy. From now on, if a prospective buyer asks for a deal, think ahead about what concession you could make that wouldn't cost much but would make them happy. A happy customer is more important than a few dollars of marginal cost. Think about the lifetime value of any customer. How much is their repeat business worth to you over a lifetime?

I have been a business coach for over thirty years, and a speaker and author for ten more years beyond that. I have seen a lot of coaching clients come and go, but I was shocked to learn that nearly 50 percent of my clients who leave come back for more coaching at some point. At the end of coaching, I always tell clients how much I've enjoyed working with them and often give them a parting gift of a new book or something else that is meaningful. I know there is a 50 percent chance they will come back.

Think of all your customers this way. Don't measure business by a single transaction; gauge it by the lifetime revenue of a business relationship.

KEY TAKEAWAYS

1. Make the other side feel good about negotiating with you.
2. Offer a small concession to make them feel good, even if you don't want to negotiate.
3. Congratulate them on their skills.
4. Tell them what a good deal they got.
5. Think about the lifetime value of a customer.

Strategy 13: How Much Will the Seller Take?

In every negotiation, the seller has a price they hope to get and one below which they will not sell. Every buyer has a deal they want and a deal from which they will walk away. Your job is to get as close to the deal you want as possible, especially before you start negotiating.

My youngest daughter, Caroline, is the most stubborn of my three girls. The older two can be scolded, cajoled, and browbeaten into behaving appropriately. But Caroline, when she was younger, would evaluate the punishment versus the behavior I was trying to discourage. For example, she was expected to do the dishes every evening. When she forgot, I would remind her by saying, "I asked you to do the dishes three times. If you don't get in the kitchen, there will be consequences."

Caroline would say, "What kind of consequences?"

I had to be careful here, because if the punishment was not severe enough, she would just take the consequence. If it was too severe—for example, grounding her for a couple days—I would get into trouble with her mother. That was Caroline's way of having me commit to the punishment first—in other words, give her my bottom line so she could start the negotiation.

Children are naturally gifted negotiators. When asked to do something, they will usually say, "What will you give me?" Or they will negotiate a penalty when they've done something wrong. This is mainly because parents want to be fair and often feel guilty if they are too harsh. Like mine, your children are able to get to the bottom line quickly. They are masters at starting the negotiation at your lowest offer. Like your kids, you need to get to the other side's bottom line quickly, albeit with more elegance and decorum.

It's always a good idea to enter a negotiation already knowing what the other side will settle for. The value of a product or service is only what both sides agree to. But any bargain can go more smoothly if you could find out in advance what that is. For example, if you want to buy a pickup truck for $10,000, but know the sticker price is $15,000, it would be good to know in advance what they will accept. It would let you know if there is any chance of negotiating a better agreement.

TAKE AWAY THEIR HIGHER AUTHORITY

Later we will talk more about how to take away the other party's *higher authority* while preserving yours. For example, it's a good idea to tell the seller you will have to check with your spouse before you can make a decision. But when the seller wants to check with somebody else, ask what they will recommend. For example, use the higher authority to find how much the seller would take: "I'm doing some shopping for my wife. She wants a robot vacuum cleaner, but I'm not sure which one to get. What's the lowest you could go on this one? I will tell her and ask what she thinks." In this case, you are not really negotiating. You're getting them to set the lowest initial price so that you can come back and start the negotiation.

PLAY THE RELUCTANT BUYER

Another way to set the stage for a low beginning price is to play the reluctant buyer: "This isn't exactly what I want. But if I did choose your service, what is the lowest you could go?"

The walkaway tactic can also be used. This tactic tells the seller that you are done. If the negotiation doesn't progress, you just walk out the door. You could also use this tactic as a way to get the seller to name their lowest price. You would simply ask, "What's the lowest price you would take for this?" Then let them know in a polite way that the price is too high, but you appreciate their time. Then walk out the door, pop back in, and say in a very polite way, "I really like that product. Is there any way you could discount it a little more?" If they say no, you can negotiate for extras and eventually work around to a lower price. But at least you know what the bottom line is, because they were willing to let you walk out the door.

These are tactics you can use to gain an opening price. But if you are a seller, you need defenses. When a buyer is checking prices for somebody else, ask to talk to the person making the decision, not the messenger. If a reluctant buyer tells you what they don't like about your product and how it is not really appropriate for them, ask what they are really looking for. If they answer, perhaps you have another product that better serves their needs and can bargain anew.

When I am signing books at speeches, an attendee will frequently ask, "I have a friend who is a meeting planner. I would love to tell her about you. Do you have a business card? How much do you charge for a speech?" Nothing good can come of my response. I either tell the person my speaking fee or refuse to tell them and risk losing the engagement. A much better response is to negotiate with the buyer instead of the messenger. I typically say, "It depends on the event. If you can give me your friend's name and contact information, I will give her a call and find out more about her goals."

All this knowledge comes from making frequent past negotiation mistakes. I've given a messenger the speaking fee. The messenger usually comes back and says they spoke to their boss, and the fee is too high; can I drop it by 25 percent? I agree. The messenger returns with a request that I drop my fee by another 10 percent and include the airfare. It's almost like a good cop, bad cop scenario. I've made the mistake of negotiating with somebody who cannot make a decision, but is trying to get an opening price. When I eventually do talk to the decision maker, I can expect more concessions to be requested.

I was at a jewelry festival many years ago, talking to the wife of my tennis partner. Her necklaces were gorgeous. Most were between $50 and $100. There were many browsers and a few buyers. One shopper said to my friend, "This necklace is beautiful. I have a friend who would love this, but she doesn't have much money. What's the least you would take for this piece?"

Like many entrepreneurs, my friend's wife would have probably given it away at cost. I stepped in and said, "Why don't you have your friend come over or call directly?" Then I said, "You could take a picture on your phone and send it to her. Then they can discuss the price directly." I think I shocked my friend's wife. I told her the messenger was using a ruse to get an opening price—one the buyer would have tried to discount later on.

KEY TAKEAWAYS

1. In the beginning, ask for the lowest price the other party would accept.
2. Don't negotiate with people who can't say yes.
3. Ask to speak to the person who can say yes directly.

2

Easy Tactics You Need to Learn

A few very simple tactics are important in any negotiation. These common-sense ideas will help you make a good deal every time.

In any negotiation, the power goes to the party who is best prepared. It's unlikely that you will read this book in the middle of a negotiation. So it's important to study these techniques first and then apply them soon as possible so that they will stick in your memory. They will help make your next negotiation even more successful.

Tactic 1: The First Offer

It's important to never make the first offer. Get the other side to tell you what they want first. This will allow you to bracket, flinch, act the reluctant buyer, and help you gain even more concessions. I recently asked my gardener the price for planting new sod. He quoted $2,600. I asked if he would do it for $1,800. We predictably bracketed to $2,200. We would not have settled on this if I had told him what my budget was or had not asked him to make the first offer.

Sometimes it's tempting to start your negotiation from a list or published price. For example, hotel publishes a rack rate of $150 a night. (A rack rate is the official or advertised rate for the room.) It would be a mistake to say, "I know your rates are $150. Would you take $100 for the room tonight?" The manager may either say yes, which would make you sorry that you didn't offer less, or counter at $125, which you would be tempted to accept.

Instead, don't assume that any published price is sacrosanct. Ask, "What is the lowest price for a room tonight?" Hotels for example, are famous for publishing rack rates that are far higher than the fee they will accept. It's much better to ignore any published prices and simply ask what their discount rate is. You can start the negotiation there.

Services like hotel rooms and golf tee times are perishable. If they are not used, they become worthless. An empty hotel room makes no money for a hotel. An empty seat on an airplane makes no money for the airline. Even some revenue for a perishable item is better than none.

I live part-time in a small southern Portuguese town called Carvoeiro, in the Algarve region. We try to stay there one month out of every three. It's such a popular cottage that it is occupied nearly year-round. At the end of one stay, we left at noon before the renters arrived at 3 p.m. The problem was that our flight from Lisbon to the US didn't leave until the next day.

So we went to the most beautiful hotel in the area, the Tivoli. It's a five-star hotel with expensive ocean views, but it is only fully occupied in the summer.

At the front desk, I asked the manager the lowest rate for a room that night. The manager quoted their $200 rack rate. I said, "I appreciate that, but what is the lowest rate you would accept for a room tonight?" He immediately discounted to $120, stating that it was a onetime exception for area residents. (It's always amazing to me that when a vendor lowers the price, they always act as if it's a one-time exception or something they never do.) I countered and said, "Would you take $100 for it tonight?"

He said, "I can't go that low, but I can put you in an ocean view room for $110. Will that be OK?"

By refusing to accept the published price and asking for the lowest price they would accept, I was able to get a $90 discount as well as an upgrade to a room with a view.

This is the power of making sure the other party makes the first offer. Starting here will usually yield better results.

Sometimes the first offer is not even about money. It's about convenience. My brother Kevin and I once had a golf tee time at 2 p.m. near Kona, Hawaii. We arrived at noon, thinking we would have lunch and practice on the driving range. We checked in a little before twelve. My brother, who is always trying to get a better deal, said, "Any chance we can get out earlier?"

The starter, realizing that an unused tee time is worth nothing, said, "Sure, you can go out anytime."

Although we didn't save money, we got home much earlier.

The starter might have asked for more money because we were playing at an earlier, more expensive time. In that case, we would have started negotiating for the best deal we could get.

Don't be afraid to get the other side to make the first offer. But also make sure their offer is the lowest available.

KEY TAKEAWAYS

1. Get the other side to make the first offer.
2. In the beginning, ask what the lowest they would take.
3. Be open to offers other than money.

Tactic 2: Declining Value of Services

It's always amazing to me how desperate people are to buy a service and how much they devalue it once it is rendered. Fifteen years ago, I was the keynote speaker at an accountants' convention in New Orleans. One CPA told me he saved a client $120,000 in taxes. He billed the client $10,000 for services rendered. The client sent a nasty letter saying he had been overcharged and thought the bill should be less. The client had been terrified of paying $120,000 in taxes, but devalued the CPA's expertise when the bill came due.

Once in a while, I will speak gratis for nonprofit groups. But I always make every group pays at least for airfare, hotel, and ground transportation.

I learned very early in my career that if you speak for free, groups treat you like a free speaker. I once gave an hour talk for the National Association of Fixed Annuities. Over 200 annuity executives were in attendance and gave me a standing ovation. The meeting was in Washington, D.C. My oldest daughter, Stacey, was chief of staff for a US congressman at the time and lived nearby. She came to my speech, making her father very happy.

Three months later, my bill for the airfare and taxi had still not been paid by the association. I called the executive, Kim, and asked what the delay was. She said some of the board members didn't want to pay for me to visit my daughter. This is a good example of declining value of services.

Realtors tell me sellers are usually very happy to pay 5 percent commission, including 2.5 percent for the buyer's agent and 2.5 percent for the seller's agent. Realtors earn their fees. They help the homeowner spruce up the house, sometimes find contractors to paint and remodel, and may even put in some time themselves cleaning up the house. When you add in their negotiation skills, the commission they charge is very fair. Yet after the house is sold, sellers often grumble about the high 5 percent fee they are charged.

A massage therapist told me recently that he was able to get a patient out of severe neck pain. He typically charges $60 an hour for therapy, but in this case, he went an extra thirty minutes and charged the relieved patient $90. After the massage, the patient questioned the higher fee.

Declining value of services frequently happens when providers go the extra mile. They do a favor, give something extra, or even make sacrifices to help the client. While this seems like great customer service, often it's not appreciated. The answer is to get a concession before you do something extra. For example, "If I organize the landscapers, can you refer me to your neighbors?" Or, "If I'm able to deliver the furniture a week early, can you pay the delivery workers in cash?" Or, "If we are able to get the IRS to decrease the tax bill, can you pay my bill within seven days instead of thirty?"

While it's natural to provide extra services to your clients and customers, it must also be appreciated. I can usually determine those who are likely to devalue favors later. These are the people most likely to request concessions. Above all, don't think that because you went over and above, the customer will make it up to you later.

Most new consultants charge a fee but overdeliver. More experienced consultants realize that the fee needs to be negotiated up front. Any extra services will be soon forgotten.

If you negotiate your service fees, be prepared that the buyer may experience declining value of services. Negotiate everything up front. Don't expect unrequited concessions later. When I sold my house in Orange County, California in February 2021, the sales price was $130,000 more than the list. Moreover, it sold in three days. The Realtor, whom I had used thirty years earlier to buy the same house, was a master negotiator. The buyers wanted more than $30,000 in repairs and other items. We settled for $10,000 in concessions. I rented the house back for two months. We rejected the request for a $5,000 security deposit. After all this, I was so impressed with my Realtor that I gave him an extra $10,000 in commission. He said in all his forty years in real estate, nobody had ever given him more than the commission agreed to up front. This is an exception. It will be rare for any of your customers to value all the extra work you did.

It's kind of like the plumber who fixed a leaky pipe in five minutes and charged the homeowner $180. Outraged, the owner said,

"I'm a surgeon, and even I don't charge people $180 for five minutes of work!" The plumber said, "Funny, when I was a surgeon, I didn't charge $180 for a five-minute procedure either."

KEY TAKEAWAYS

1. Any service you provide will be discounted later.
2. Negotiate up front any extra services or products.
3. Never expect nonnegotiated concessions from the other side.

Tactic 3: Dumb Is Smart

Do you remember the 1970s detective series *Colombo*? The title character, played by Peter Falk, continually seemed not to understand what the suspect was saying. He always acted dumb. In fact, he would often walk out the door, come back in, and say, "Let me get this straight . . ." Then he would ask the suspect a question that would crack the case.

If you want to be a great negotiator, you should never make assumptions about what the other side said. You should always painstakingly clarify.

One of my friends contracted a bathroom remodel. He was quoted $12,000 and negotiated the completion date and materials. He thought he had negotiated fixture prices, but the contractor had actually budgeted for a lower-quality product. Like Colombo, he said, "Of course you will install Kohler hardware, right?" The contractor said he'd have to charge more. My friend flinched, and the contractor relented. What you heard may not be what they said. It is critical in any negotiation to clarify and get agreement.

RECAP AND CLARIFY

One of the biggest mistakes in any negotiation is making assumptions. We assume a delivery will be on time or the other party will absorb extra charges. We assume payment terms. We assume first-class airfare and ground transportation reimbursement. We assume the start date will be in the next few days. All these assumptions should be dealt with in the very beginning. A great way to do this is to recap and clarify. Recapping is saying, "Let me get this straight." Clarifying is saying, "If I understand you correctly, you want X. Did I get that right, or is there something more?"

The older we get, the more experienced we become. I have made assumptions about mileage costs. I didn't get reimbursed for driving my own car to a speaking engagement. Because I didn't negotiate ground transportation from the airport to the hotel, the taxi charge was an extra that I had to pay. Because I didn't negotiate a break for a speech, I lost thousands of dollars in audio and video product sales. Because I didn't negotiate a recording of my presentation, the client planned to give my speech free to all the attendees. When I tried to negotiate a fee for this after the agreement, hard feelings ensued.

Dumb is smart. We tend to help those who have lots of questions. We tend not to take advantage of those who ask for clarification, and we go slow. Those negotiators who act confident and move quickly are often the ones who make the most mistakes.

I moved to Daniel Island, South Carolina, in the summer of 2021. My family came to visit for the month of August. We needed a king-size mattress for the guest room. At the mattress store, we found one California king bed that was especially comfortable.

Before we settled on price, I asked questions about everything I could think of. Did the frame come with the mattress? How is the mattress protected from stains? How often does it need to be flipped without developing lumps? Do I need to have a topper on it? How soon will it be delivered? How much is the cost for delivery?

I have purchased many mattresses in my life and had a good idea of what to expect. But as I asked these questions, the salesperson was more than willing to throw in all the extras. For example, shipping was free. The frame would be included. The delivery time was cut in half. After all this, we finally negotiated a 30 percent discount from the lowest price they would accept. None of this would have happened if I had acted confident and moved quickly through the purchase. Because I took my time and appeared uninformed, I got a much better deal that I would have otherwise.

KEY TAKEAWAYS
1. Always get total clarity on every part of the deal.
2. Never make assumptions about the other side.
3. Recap and clarify every relevant point.

Tactic 4: Read and Write the Whole Agreement

If your negotiation ends with a written agreement, make sure you read every word. Something may have slipped in benefiting the other side.

Verbal negotiations are only part of the agreement. The written contract usually includes many details the other side didn't think of in the verbal discussions. It is better to write a brief memorandum after any verbal agreement; that way, you both can see what you agreed to, and the agreement can be straightforward.

Recently I agreed to decrease my speaking fee for a group in Salt Lake City. As a concession, they agreed to purchase books for the whole audience. But when I read the agreement, a line was slipped in. It said that any of my educational materials would be sold through their conference bookstore, which would take a 25 percent commission. Much of my speaking income comes from books, videos, and CDs. If a group tells me up front that product sales aren't allowed, I usually increase my speaking fee. If I hadn't noticed this change in the agreement, it would have decreased revenue from the event.

Now when I read any agreement, I automatically assume any changes will be to the other side's advantage. If you can read agreements with that expectation, you will be much better prepared. Assume that any agreement will not be to your benefit.

Many negotiations between countries were substantially changed from the verbal agreement when written. Donald Trump's administration imposed substantial tariffs on a broad array of Chinese goods. Trump not only tried to stop the theft of intellectual property but also tried to get China to open up more of its economy to American goods. An agreement was reached, called "a framework of understanding." The stock market hit new highs and many nations were relieved by this agreement. Then the Chinese delegation changed the written agreement just before formal signing, reversing nearly all of the concessions. The enthusiasm from both sides led each to believe that a verbal agreement was reached, when there were still substantial differences, as logged in the written agreement.

In the 1970s, negotiations between the administrations of Israel's Menachem Begin and Egypt's president Anwar Sadat led to an agreement called the Camp David Accords, mediated by US president Jimmy Carter. Begin was so proud that he told his wife history was made—until Egypt changed the written agreement, making it impossible for Israel to sign.

PAY ATTENTION TO CHANGES

It takes a lot of discipline to read an agreement every time there is a change. It's far easier to pay attention only to the changes rather than to the whole contract. But that is exactly what you need to do. When I was selling my house, I reread the agreement, which I had already seen a few times. I noticed that the buyers now wanted to extend the escrow to sixty days. It was tempting to review only what I thought were changes. Even my Realtor didn't catch them.

It is also tempting to let your representative, such as your Realtor, read through any changes. After all, they see these contracts every day. You don't have the experience, but you still need to read and review it all every time. It will be tedious, but it is necessary. It's true that if mistakes were made, you could sue your Realtor or attorney for malpractice. But there is no guarantee that you will win. It could also take years and cost a lot to prevail. In the age of Docusign, it's easy to just scan the agreement online instead of printing it out and discussing it.

In 2019, I bought a house in the Algarve region of Portugal. Lawyers are used for all property transactions in Portugal. After the verbal agreement between me and the selling Realtor, my lawyer wrote up the contract for me to read and sign. No problem, except that it was all in Portuguese. I can speak basic tourist Portuguese, but nothing more. I had to translate every word of a twenty-page agreement. It took me weeks of reading and lots of calls to my lawyer. It was helpful that the sellers were British and my attorney spoke fluent English. But it could have been disastrous if something slipped by that I didn't know about. Imagine suing someone in another country!

These days, any verbal agreement I make is followed by a written note to the other side. If I do a deal with a computer repair technician, I will follow it with an email about our conversation. If a car repair tech quotes me a price for an oil change, I will send an email back outlining the price, the type of oil, and even the date of repair and completion. If you think this is excessive, think about how much a misunderstanding could cost.

OFFER TO WRITE THE AGREEMENT

If you really want to avoid any surprises, write your own agreements to memorialize the negotiation. When I speak, we have a standard agreement outlining basic things like hotel, date, time, speaking fee, airfare, and ground transportation. If a client changes anything, it is instantly flagged. Then we can go back to the client and ask for further concessions. Sometimes a client will write in their plan that they will record my presentation on video, so I have to go back and negotiate a higher price. Sometimes the client will write in a longer speaking time instead of what we agreed to. I then need to flag the change and ask for a concession. Always write the agreement, and read it all after any changes.

KEY TAKEAWAYS
1. Offer to write the agreement.
2. Read the whole agreement every time.
3. Expect unexpected changes when the agreement comes back.

Tactic 5: Decreasing Value of Concessions

The biggest concessions are always made at the end of a negotiation, especially when there's time pressure. During the failed attempt to repeal Obamacare in March 2017, the conservative Freedom Caucus was able to gain the biggest concessions from House speaker Paul Ryan and the Trump administration, but only in the last few days. The repeal didn't pass because the Freedom Caucus tried to act the reluctant buyer and nibbled too much at the end. The late Arizona senator John McCain cast the deciding vote against the Freedom Caucus's demands.

As we have discussed often in this book, there are many ways of getting a better deal. Flinching, the reluctant buyer or seller, and bracketing are just some techniques that we've talked about. Some deals take too long and become less valuable as you make more concessions. It's important to let the other side know that any further negotiations won't yield much more benefit. The way to do this is to make increasingly small concessions as the negotiation progresses.

Forcing a decision in this way is called *decreasing value of concessions*. If the other side makes a demand, you yield a concession that not much better than the last offer. If you bracket the other side, make your next concession very close to your last one. The benefit to decreasing your concession is that the other side will realize there is little benefit to keep negotiating. It will shorten the time of the negotiation and bring it to a conclusion faster.

For example, you want to buy a house. You and the seller are $50,000 apart. The seller wants $600,000 for the house. You bracket by offering $500,000, hoping to buy it for $550,000. At first the seller seems reluctant and counters at $575,000. You move your offer up to $540,000. The seller makes another concession at $560,000—still not where you want to be, at $550,000. You don't want this to go on forever and put some pressure on the seller. You offer $545,000: only slightly more than your last concession. That signals the seller that they'd better make a bigger concession, or the negotiation is done; there's no further motivation on your part to offer more money.

Here is another example. You want to buy a used car. The other side decreased their sales price from $40,000 to $35,000, and you want to pay $20,000. You can increase your counteroffer to $22,000. This will stop them from bracketing you to the middle. But it will also signal an end to the negotiation. You'd better be prepared to walk away from a bad deal.

A building contractor I play tennis with told me a story about negotiating a kitchen remodel. He wanted $50,000, but the homeowners only wanted to pay $40,000. He went down to $45,000, and they went up to $42,000. But instead of bracketing, he offered to diminish the concession by saying he would personally supervise the project. He probably would have done that anyway. But at least the homeowners knew the price concessions were over.

The tactic of decreasing value of concessions only means the money part of the negotiation is over. Perhaps we can negotiate something else that is palatable. Just as the building contractor stopped the price from going lower and offered a different kind of concession, you can make a concession in another area.

One client asked for a 25 percent decrease in my speaking fee. I countered by offering to include my airfare in the fee. This particularly insistent client asked if I would decrease my speaking fee by 20 percent and also include the air travel expenses. I was done making financial concessions. I offered something else instead. I said, "You plan on having a cocktail party the evening before my speech?" They said yes. I said, "Often my clients find it valuable for the keynote speaker to attend a gathering the evening before the speech. Would that be beneficial to you?" After they said yes, I said, "Great! I will include that without charge." They agreed, and we booked the program.

I usually fly into a city between 6 and 9 p.m. on the day before my speech, because airlines are so unpredictable and I want to get some rest before a speaking event. It was very easy for me to take a slightly earlier flight and be available for a 6 p.m. reception. But the client knew that financial concessions were at an end. If they pocketed my attendance to the cocktail party and still asked for a lower speaking fee, I would have walked away.

There is a common mindset in the professional speaking industry that one should never negotiate a speaking fee. The thought is that if any others hear you did a presentation for less than the published fee, it diminishes your credibility. I disagree. There are always speakers who are willing to charge less money than me. Besides, the actual speech is only part of the total revenue from the engagement. There are also sales of audios, videos, and other products. There are potential coaching engagements as well as referrals to other groups. I look at the total benefit of the meeting instead of the speaking fee alone. Most presenters look solely at the fee and nothing else.

Plus, I enjoy negotiation. I like using these techniques and skills. It's fun when an attendee asks after a presentation if I will accept 50 percent less for my books or audiovisual programs. Instead of saying no, as most presenters would, I bracket and ask for concessions. I have fun in the process.

If there is a line of people waiting to buy my books and they hear that one of them was able to get a 50 percent discount, they may ask for the same deal. To deflect that, I ask for the person requesting the discount to wait until later so I can talk to them privately. Even then, I will never simply give a discount without getting some type of concession.

Be prepared to make concessions increasingly small if you want to end the negotiation. Signal to the other side that they should accept your offer, or you will walk away. Of course, forcing a decision could go either way. They may say yes or no, but at least you can get to the end of the negotiation.

KEY TAKEAWAYS

1. Decrease the value of your concessions to signal that the negotiation is at an end.
2. Make concessions in another area of value instead of price.
3. Be willing to negotiate everything, regardless of the conventional wisdom. Make the experience enjoyable. Have fun.

Tactic 6: The Red Herring

Have you ever wanted to negotiate but weren't sure about how much room you had to deal? Have you ever wanted to buy at the lowest price, but weren't prepared to walk away? You really wanted the item, no matter what, but still wanted to get the best deal you could?

The answer might be to employ the *red herring* technique: negotiating for an item that you never intended to buy. It's a tactic to find out how much room the other side has in making concessions. It is simply negotiating the best deal available and walking away. This will give you an idea of how much the other side is willing to give up. It will indicate what they will also give up on the product that you really want to buy.

Let's say that you want to buy a brand-name king-size mattress. The price is $2,000. You get the store manager to make the first offer. You ask the lowest price he is willing to take. He says $1,750, to which you counter at $1,500. You both bracket to the middle at $1,625. Now you know that the manager is willing to give up about 20 percent on the retail price without much effort. But now you know there are more concessions available. Will the manager throw in the box springs? Will he also include the metal frame? How about the extended warranty? How about a free delivery within seven days? You can even ask about extra remote controls for a reclining bed. The manager says yes to everything except for the remote controls. Now you know the extent of the concessions that are available: a 20 percent discount with lots of extras.

But here's the twist. You've just negotiated a great deal on a bed you didn't want to buy. You simply say, "I'm not sure this bed is the right one for me after all. How about that California king in the corner? I tried it out, and it seems much better for me." There's a high likelihood that the bed you do want to buy also has a 20 percent discount. It also has many extras that could be included at no cost.

What if the manager doesn't want to give you a 20 percent discount on the California king? He only offers 10 percent because the supply is limited. You simply respond, "That's too bad, because you gave me a 20 percent discount on the other bed." The manager would be hard-pressed to refuse the discount since he offered it to you on the red herring.

I recently bought a new Wilson Clash tennis racket from my club in Daniel Island, South Carolina. I asked what the price was for the Wilson Clash tour racket, which I did not want to buy. The vendor said, "$175, but since you are a tennis club member, I will give you a 25 percent discount."

I said, "How about a 35 percent discount?"

The vendor agreed immediately and even offered to throw in new strings: a $30 value. But the racket I really wanted to buy was the Wilson Clash regular, which was much more popular. I said, "On second thought, the tour has a bigger frame and is less suited for my game. How about making the same deal for the Clash regular racket?"

He said, "We only have a few of these, and I'm not sure I could make you the same deal."

"I understand," I said. "I really want that racket; I guess I'll buy it online instead."

He immediately agreed to the deal, and I walked out with the racket I really wanted by negotiating for the racket I did not want.

The red herring works so well because of momentum. When someone negotiates, they tend to want to reach a conclusion. They often rationalize why even a marginal deal is better than none at all. If I had tried to negotiate for the Wilson Clash regular, the vendor would have pushed back, saying they were in short supply; any racket he had would probably sell soon. But since I got him to negotiate on a racket he really wanted to sell, I found out how much room there was in the negotiation and the concessions he would make. The momentum of the negotiation also drew him into extending the same deal for a more valuable tennis racket.

In 2015, I bought a used, six-month-old Porsche Cayenne S SUV. The great part was the price. The dealer gave it to me for 20 percent less than the sticker. He accepted my offer immediately, so I probably could have bought this car for less. I planned on bracketing. But it was accepted so quickly that I will never know how low they would have gone.

The real story is about the red herring I negotiated before buying this car. There was another Cayenne on the lot, about one-year-old. It was slightly less expensive than the model S that I wanted. I offered 25 percent below sticker price. The dealer pushed back and said they couldn't go below 20 percent. I also asked about a discount on the extended warranty, which he agreed to. I asked that a special protective film be put on the front end to protect against chips and bug damage. He also agreed to that.

But then I walked away and said the Cayenne S was more powerful; I especially liked the twin turbo engine better. I offered 20 percent below sticker price, which the dealer agreed to. But I then asked if he would still give me the extras that were available on the car I did not want. He agreed to that. I left money and concessions on the table because the dealer accepted my offer without countering. I should have offered 25 percent less instead of 20 percent to find out the dealer's walkaway price. But I did find out fairly quickly how much room he had to negotiate. There was no downside, since I was also prepared to walk away at any time.

Use the red herring on any major negotiation. It is unlikely to work on custom real estate properties or private party cars and boats. But if the seller has a few choices, negotiate for an item that you don't want in order to find out the bottom line on the purchase you do want to make. You won't be obligated to make the deal, but you will be very confident about what kind of deal you can get.

KEY TAKEAWAYS

1. Negotiate on an item you don't want in order to find out what kind of deal you can get on something you do want.

2. Even if your purchase is more valuable than the red herring, the momentum from the last negotiation will produce a better deal on the item you want.

3. Since you walked away from the red herring, the seller will know that you could walk away from the new purchase also. You are likely to get an equal or better deal on the purchase you want.

Tactic 7: Forcing a Decision

Do your negotiations seem to drag on? Would you like a negotiation to proceed more quickly? You can force a decision more quickly by employing some useful tactics. One is time pressure. Another is competition.

We've already discussed shortening a negotiation through decreasing the value of concessions. As we move even more slowly toward what the other party wants, they get the impression that the negotiation has little more room to go. But there are other techniques you can use to make the deal progress more quickly.

I don't like to put pressure on people to make a decision, but I do want to know about the pressure they are under. At the same time, I want to minimize any pressure on me. The two most common areas of pressure are *time* and *competition*.

TIME PRESSURE

When one side has time pressure, they tend to lose power and make more concessions. I speak to car dealers often. Sometimes their quotas are quarterly, but their pressure can still be intense at the end of the month. If you negotiate a price in the first week of a month, you are unlikely to get as good a deal as in the last few days.

Remember we spoke about price, timing, and quality? If you need to buy a car today, you will lose options and make concessions.

It's very useful to find out what the other side's deadline is, but never give them yours. During the initial conversation, I often ask when they have to make a decision. I know I have a better chance of gaining concessions if they are in a time crunch.

Frequently people will be quite candid in talking about their weaknesses and anxieties. If you ask what someone's deadline is, they are often willing to say, "Last week," or, "By Friday." But when I am asked about deadlines, I always say I don't have one. Even if you have a deadline, never tell the other side what it is. Always say, "I'm in no rush."

It is tempting to think that you always have the weaker hand in a negotiation. That is probably not true. You don't know if there are any other buyers. They may be time-pressured to do a deal with you. You also don't know what their expenses are in waiting for someone with a better deal. You have no idea about the anxiety level of the other side. Don't assume that you have more pressure than them.

One way to introduce time pressure during a stalled negotiation is to look at your watch and say, "I have to go. I have an appointment right now and can't spend any more time on this." The other side will likely make one more offer to keep you there a few more minutes. You need to be prepared to walk away if they don't, but you can always come back later and accept the last offer.

Introducing time pressure is always a good idea to get the negotiation restarted or to move faster.

A good way to find out if they have time pressure is to simply ask. Often they will let you know. A crafty way is asking at the beginning of the meeting, "How are we doing for time?" The other party will usually say, "I'm OK; I've got time." Or they may say, "I have a meeting in an hour, but I have time to talk until then." This way you can elegantly find out what their time pressure is. Just be aware that the biggest concessions will be made in the last ten minutes of your negotiation.

My daughter Stacey worked as chief of staff for two US congressmen. She was also press secretary for the governor of Virginia. Until recently, she was lobbyist with a major firm in Washington, D.C. Now she is vice president of communications and government affairs with a Utah-based ski resort company. Stacey frequently tells me about the negotiation tactics politicians use to extract concessions. Time pressure is one of the most popular.

The debt ceiling needs to be raised about once a year to accommodate extra spending by Congress. The Republicans tend to want to decrease deficits by making small ceiling raises. The Democrats want to spend more and therefore vote for bigger debt ceiling raises. No matter the motivation, agreements usually occur within about an hour before any deadline shuts down the government. This happened during Barack Obama's administration as well as during Donald Trump's. It will also happen in ensuing administrations. Once a deadline is missed, each side tries to put renewed time pressure on the other. They point out the number of government workers who are unable to pay their mortgages. They trot out business owners who depend on the government and advertise how close they are to bankruptcy. All this is an attempt to introduce more time pressure on the other side.

One of the most extreme examples of time pressure was in 1994, during the Clinton administration. Former president Jimmy Carter traveled to Haiti with Senator Sam Nunn and Colin Powell, the joint chief of staff. Their mission was to persuade dictator Raoul Cédras to leave the country. The US government threat, conveyed by Carter, was that if Cédras did not leave, the US would invade Haiti. At the end of the second day of negotiations, President Clinton called Carter and told him to leave the country: Haiti would be invaded in the next thirty minutes. Cédras left the country at once. Can you imagine the degree of pressure you would feel knowing in the next thirty minutes your country would be invaded and you would be put in jail, probably for the rest of your life?

My brother Kevin was able to buy a new Corvette for the invoice price. He utilized the dealer's time pressure to get the deal he wanted. Whenever Kevin buys a car, he always asks for the invoice. Surprisingly, dealers always show it to him. If I sold cars for a living, I would be hesitant to disclose my actual costs.

Kevin said, "I will give you the price on the invoice, but no more. I'm in no rush. Anytime you want to call me, I'm ready to do the deal." Kevin said this to a few dealers at the beginning of the month. But he knew that most dealers felt pressure at the end of the month.

Sure enough, this tactic worked. Kevin hosted a pool party for some friends and their kids. The dealer called him and said he was ready to sell for the price on the invoice. Kevin responded that he was in the middle of hosting a party and asked the dealer to bring the paperwork to his house as well as the new Corvette.

Surprisingly, the manager brought the Corvette to Kevin's house, with the paperwork. I have purchased many cars in my life, but never has a dealer brought the car and the paperwork to my house. That's the power of time pressure. The dealer had to sell the car that day.

COMPETITION PRESSURE

Another way to force a decision is introducing competition. Remember, the side that has more options is always in a position of power. The side with fewer options has less power. If you are a house flipper and tell the other side you are considering other properties, you will gain more concessions.

Competition pressure works in nearly every area of negotiation. Telling a car dealer that a model is less expensive at a competitor is one way. Explaining to a store that a website has the same model and will deliver faster is another way. Unless a vendor has too much business and is looking to reduce sales, they will be sensitive to competition. At first, they may tell you the competitor is deficient in some way, saying, for example, that the competitor may promise a faster delivery but rarely performs. They may disparage the competitor by saying the price will increase at the end. Don't be swayed by this tactic. It's the only argument they can make to deter you from a superior deal.

While we were still living in California, my daughter Catherine visited us. The cheapest and most frequent flights are from Los Angeles. The Orange County airport is much more expensive. But

LAX was fifty miles away from our house in Orange County. It can take two hours one way in rush-hour traffic. We usually dropped our kids off at the Disneyland hotel for the Disney Resort bus to LAX. On one occasion, the bus was twenty minutes late, and Catherine was getting nervous about making her flight.

The Super Shuttle bus was already there. I asked the driver how much he would charge for a one-way trip. He said $35. Without telling him about Catherine's time pressure, I said the Disney Resort bus would be here in a few minutes, but if he would take $20, I would put Catherine on his van instead. Of course he said yes. I introduced competition but didn't tell him about my own time pressure. This gave us more power and caused him to make a price concession.

If the Super Shuttle driver had the negotiation skills you have learned, he would have responded in a different way. He may have offered a very small concession of $34. He may also have made no concession at all to see if we would walk away. Once we did, he could have made a concession on the spot. But as we discussed earlier, an unused seat on a bus is worthless. Any amount a customer pays is better.

A client asked me to speak at a conference in Cleveland. At the end of our initial conversation about his goals, he said he was considering two other speakers for the meeting. He was trying to introduce competition into the conversation, forcing a concession from me.

At the same time, I wanted to take away competition pressure. I said, "There are other speakers who can do a good job. But it's always a risk until you use them for your group. Since you've worked with me before and had great results, wouldn't you rather use me for this meeting also? Your producers have already used my ideas to increase production. Or does it really matter to you who the presenter is?"

"Of course I'd rather use you," he said. "We have a good relationship."

My client could have put himself in more of a position of power if he had wanted to. He could have gotten me to lower the speaking fee, include airfare, or grant even deeper concessions, depending on how badly I wanted to speak to his group. But he will never know, because he never followed through on the competition pressure.

KEY TAKEAWAYS

1. Find out the other party's time and competition pressure. Don't talk about yours.
2. The most concessions are made in the last 20 percent of the negotiation. Let the other side know that you have to leave in a few minutes if it's not moving quickly enough.
3. Tell the other side about competition. Let them know about other offers.

Tactic 8: Monopoly Money

One of the strangest tactics I have ever heard of is when the other side negotiates with *play money*. This is often used in real estate discussions to make you think the price is less than it really is. For example, a mortgage broker might tell you the loan will only cost an extra $20 per day. That doesn't seem like a lot of money until you consider that it's actually $600 per month. Car dealers love to say that buying a newer model will only cost an extra $10 per day. They'll also tell you the fuel economy savings of 35 miles per gallon instead of 20 will offset any extra price you pay for the more expensive car.

Don't fall for this. Dollars are dollars, whether you pay them daily, monthly, or yearly. I expect at some point this could get truly ridiculous. Eventually some dealer may quote a cost as only 80 cents more per hour.

We are very vulnerable to play money claims. Term life insurance premiums are only $3 a day. Who can't afford $3 a day? An upgraded, premium, extended warranty is only an extra 75 cents per day. This is not even as expensive as a cup of coffee.

Yet play money can also be beneficial. Thinking of an affordable amount of money that can be directed to another purpose, like a savings plan, is an easy mental exercise. Financial writer Jonathan Pond once pointed that putting $3.95 into a jar every day instead of buying one Starbucks coffee would earn you $600,000 in 30 years. When I told my daughter Caroline about this plan, she started her retirement savings the next day.

Play money isn't just breaking cost down to days or hours. It can also be a promise of things to come. Many years ago, I let myself get trapped by this play money gambit, although my error did not involve actual money. My play money error was believing an insincere promise. A manager with the New England Insurance Company promised that if I would drop my speaking fee by 50 percent, he would book me for three more regional meetings. Since he was the planner for those events, I dropped my fee.

After the speech, the manager told me what a great job I did. I reminded him of the promise to book me for the regional meetings. The manager went silent. He failed to return any phone calls. I should have made the other three engagements part of the original deal instead of just accepting a promise. (Of course, the more we negotiate, the more experience and smarter we get.)

This could also be an example of declining value of services. The manager was desperate to get a great speaker. Unfortunately, he probably didn't have the budget. He made a big promise he probably never intended to keep. This happens a lot in negotiation. The other party says, "If you give me a great deal now, I'll make sure that you get all our business later." A more obvious play money promise would be, "If you give me a discount today, I will tell all my friends about you." This is unlikely to happen. You can think of it as fake Monopoly money.

Customer research has shown that a satisfied customer will tell three others about their experience (while an unsatisfied customer will tell twelve others). Even if you do a good job, it's unlikely that the customer will keep their promise of telling others any more than would a satisfied customer who didn't make the promise.

KEY TAKEAWAYS

1. Don't fall for gimmicks that makes the price seem lower than it really is.
2. Monopoly money can take the form of promises that are not kept.

3. Keep your focus on the outcome of the deal. Don't get distracted by the gimmicks.

Tactic 9: Requests for Proposals (RFPs)

Have you ever been asked for a request for a proposal (RFP)? You may be among ten to compete. The lowest bidder will win. Sometimes the client will use *fluffing*. This means they've already made their selection but have to abide by RFP rules prompting them to get bids from others.

In 2017, billionaire Peter Thiel, a Silicon Valley venture capitalist, presented an RFP bid to the Department of Defense (DOD) to revamp their data analytics systems for $100 million. Instead the DOD purchased a $6 billion system that was grossly inferior to the less expensive one offered by Thiel. General Dynamics, which won the bid, had political connections, enabling them to win the bid over the cheaper but more efficient options.

How did an inferior and higher priced solution win over better alternatives? Perhaps the winning bid wasn't clearly defined in the RFP. It may not have been intended to be awarded to the cheapest provider or even to the best solution. The reason for the award may not be known to the bidders.

The answer here is to clarify and get commitment to every aspect of the RFP in writing. Ask the buyer to put in writing how each decision in the RFP will be made. Is it based on price? Is it based on quality? Is it based on delivery schedule? This will put you on a more even playing field. It's much more difficult to fluff when the decision points are clear.

My friend Tony Parinello once worked for Hewlett-Packard. As I mentioned, once the provost of my alma mater, University of California at San Diego, published an RFP, inviting three of the world's biggest computer companies to bid. The provost said the award would be made to the company offering the lowest bid. The RFP suggested a $6 million system. In the 1970s, this was big money. But Tony realized Hewlett-Packard could never compete just on price and declined to bid. The provost asked Tony why he was leaving. Tony said, "You aren't considering the long-term cost. Price is what you pay right now; cost is what you pay over the long run." The provost rewrote the RFP, including not only the price but also the cost for the system over a ten-year period. Tony won the bid and made $100,000 in commission.

When you get an RFP, don't take it at face value. Call the client and get clarification on every aspect.

KEY TAKEAWAYS

1. When dealing with RFPs, always talk directly to the decision maker.
2. Find out what the decision is really based on. It's not always money.
3. Remember to discuss price versus cost in any RFP conversation.

Tactic 10: The Higher Authority

In the initial phase of every negotiation, I will ask, "Who besides you will make the final decision?" The planner will often give me the name of the program chair. At the end of the call, I offer to send one of my books to both the planner and the program chair. Then I ask for a follow-up appointment with both. During that call, I will say, "My speaking fee is $12,000. Is that within your budget?" Once I have the decision maker on the phone, the negotiation can start.

Typically, I find out during the first phone call whether there is a budget for speakers. I will ask what their budget is and how much they paid their keynote speaker last year. If they paid a small amount of $500 to $1,000, I will pass on the gig. But I will always get them to make the first offer by telling me what their budget is. The worst outcome is to have the initial phone call with an executive director or assistant who says, "I will run this by my committee," or "I'll check with my boss." This always goes badly. She will usually sell me poorly by saying to her boss or committee, "The speaker wants $12,000. Do you want to pay this much?" She will not describe my background, groups I've spoken to in the past, or any details on my credibility. She will also never mention why I'm better than all the other speakers they are considering. It's critical for me to get the decision maker on the phone and present myself.

THE TRIAL CLOSE

Part of the problem is that the planner can still resort to a higher authority. They could say, "I will run this by our committee and let you know." The best response is to get their agreement. The best way to do this is called the *trial close*. This is a temperature gauge of how warm they are at that moment. It is also a way to gain an idea of what they are concerned about. If they say, "We love it," you're probably in good shape. But if they say, "I don't know; I'll check with my committee," you have a lot more work to do.

Another trial close is, "From what you know right now, what do you think?" Or you can ask, "What will be your recommendation?" Usually they'll be honest and say there's another speaker they want for less money. Or they've already picked a speaker and just wanted to check around.

APPEAL TO THEIR EGO

One of my speaker friends will remove the higher authority by saying, "If we could accomplish all your goals, will you recommend this to your committee?" While I like this approach, it just begs for the chance to avoid discomfort by saying yes. Sometimes you can say, "Is your committee likely to follow your recommendations?" Or you can be more direct and say, "You'll recommend this, won't you?"

Years ago, I spoke to a meeting planner who seemed very excited about my topic. She said they were in the middle of picking a keynote speaker. I didn't feel I needed to employ any of these tactics, because she was so sold on me. After many voicemails, she finally called back and said her committee had picked a speaker two weeks ago, and she had been planning to call and let me know.

Rule number one is, never present to someone who can't buy, such as servers or airline workers.

But you can probe and find needs. You need to present and expect an answer from the decision maker, who *can* buy. It's critical to get them to be honest. Isn't it better to get a no rather than

wasting your time? (Isn't bad breath better than no breath at all?)
I'd much rather have somebody say that my speaking fee is out
of their budget than make me follow up five times without any
response. If you're negotiating sales of real estate, computers, or
cars, wouldn't it be better to get people to tell you no instead of
chasing them? With a stall, you're spending a lot of time following
up, only to get a no later.

THE UP-FRONT CLOSE

The best way to avoid a stall is the *up-front close*. This gets the other
side to negotiate instead of making you waste your time by chasing
them. Nothing good comes from a stall. We forget 70 percent of
what we see or hear in one day. Even worse, we forget 90 percent
after three days. If the other side of the negotiation waits more
than three days, they are unlikely to remember anything about
your product or services. But they are very likely to procrastinate
making a decision. You end up leaving multiple voicemail mes-
sages without a response. When you finally get them on the phone,
they are likely to say, "I meant to call you a while ago. We decided
to go with another vendor."

This is not because the other side has made a cogent decision.
It is because they remember more about the competitor they spoke
with recently. Think of it this way. Let's say all the follow-up dials,
voicemails, and emails cost you one hour. If your income amounts
to $100 an hour, that means you have taken a $100 bill and thrown
it in the trash. Wouldn't it be better to get someone to say no while
you are with them than taking $100 out of your pocket and throw-
ing it away?

The way to avoid this waste of time is the up-front close, such as: "If we come up with something that works for you, I hope you'll say, 'Great, let's do it.' If we come up with a plan that does not work, I hope you just say no. I'd rather you didn't say, 'Give me a few weeks or a few months.' Because that tells me you don't have all the information you need to make an informed decision. You won't hurt my feelings by saying no. Is that OK with you?" You can change these words to fit your personality, but it's critical to give the other side permission to be candid so you can start the negotiation. I use this approach whenever I talk to a coaching candidate or negotiating a speaking fee. You can adapt it to any negotiation. I'd always rather negotiate than get no for an answer, but if I do get someone to say no, I am grateful. They've avoided wasting my time, so I can work on more profitable activities.

Sometimes the other side will say they can't make a decision right now. You will of course, ask questions about their reluctance and find out more about the timing of their decision and other competitors.

Personally, I would never negotiate with someone who isn't ready, but I will present a 30,000-foot overview. For example, a Realtor might discuss how different they are from other Realtors. A car salesperson would talk about how their service is better than that of all other competitors.

The most valuable benefit of the up-front close is finding out whether the other party has to take your proposal to a committee. It also enables you to find out who the head or chair of that committee is. Then you have the chance to include that person in the final presentation.

Master negotiators only present to people who can do a deal. They don't present to assistants or administrators. They realize that presenting to someone who can't make a decision is a waste of time.

KEY TAKEAWAYS

1. Take away their higher authority, but keep yours.
2. Ask if you can talk directly to the decision maker.
3. Do the up-front close and ask if they can make a decision: yes or no.

Tactic 11: Can You Walk Away?

In the Build Back Better legislative proposal negotiations of 2021, West Virginia senator Joe Manchin and Arizona senator Kyrsten Sinema were the most visible holdouts blocking the legislation. The proposal had a price tag of $1.7 trillion, but the Congressional Budget Office scored it as nearly $5 trillion, including ten years of expenditures instead of three years. Senator Manchin was concerned about increasing the national debt and putting inflation on overdrive. Furthermore, nearly 70 percent of West Virginia voters were against the budget increases. Manchin negotiated with White House staff consistently over six months, but they would never give him the concessions West Virginia voters demanded. Instead of splitting the difference in accepting concessions his voters didn't want, Manchin walked away. The surprising part of the story was that Sen. Manchin was a dependable part of the Democratic majority. He voted with his party nearly all the time. But he chose to walk away unless he received the concessions he demanded.

Political analysts suppose that five or six other Democratic senators were also against the legislation. They were not put on record, so we will never know.

It takes courage to walk away from a deal that is not right. You also need to be able to walk away from a deal that isn't right for you.

Perhaps the most important part of any negotiation is whether you can walk away. Are you so desperate that you have to make the deal at any cost? If you fall in love with the service or product, you will pay more. If you can walk away and have options, you will always get the deal you want.

In 1991, when my daughter Catherine was born, my wife was keen on buying a safe car for our family. She loved the Volvo brand and wouldn't consider any other car. We saw a station wagon at the dealership. She looked at the price and said, "That's a great deal." I got sticker shock. She wasn't exactly the reluctant buyer I wanted. The salesperson started closing by asking how we wanted to pay for the car. I tugged my wife's arm and said, "Let's go talk about it." I explained that there were other options.

A few years ago, I wrote *Why Smart People Make Dumb Mistakes with Their Money*. In the chapter "Confirmation Bias," I point out that when people fall in love with a car brand, they tend to repeat the purchase of that same brand. We lease a car every three years and buy one every five. If you buy the same brand, you will negotiate less effectively and pay an average of $7,500 more than if you had chosen another brand.

I explained this to Merita, and we bought a Mazda MPV minivan. I jokingly say that after three daughters, it's a multipregnancy vehicle.

It's critical for you to be able to walk away from any deal that isn't right. Donald Trump was known in his private business life as a great negotiator, but he only did 10 percent of the deals he wanted. He walked away from 90 percent, because they weren't the right ones. Can you walk away? Can you turn your back and head for the door? If not, you will never get a good deal—only the one the other side is willing to offer.

After reading this book, I hope you are motivated to immediately try every tactic, especially being prepared to walk away. When I first learned about these techniques, I tried them at the Grand Bazaar in the heart of Istanbul, right next to the Bosporus, which separates Asia from Europe. I was completely outmatched by these Turkish master negotiators, but I still got good deals, because I often walked away.

One store had a full-length rabbit coat that I knew my wife would love. The price was $600, which I thought was fair. But I was so anxious to try the walkaway tactic that I risked losing it. But then I remembered if I walked out of the store and came back a few hours later, I could still get the same price. There was nothing to lose. I offered $250. The store owner countered with $400. I countered with $275, but the owner wouldn't budge. We talked for a few more minutes, and I flinched, shaking my head and looking down at the floor. My brother and I turned and headed towards the door and walked out. I looked at my brother and said, "I really want that coat. Let's go have lunch and come back and buy it."

Just then, the owner stepped out of the store and motioned for us to come back. He would take the $275 but didn't want to give me the luxury box to put it in. I smiled and stuffed it in a paper bag. I made $325 in ten minutes of negotiating. You can too, but you have to be able to walk away. These days, I'm disappointed when I can't negotiate. It's as much about the process as it is about getting a good price.

It is very difficult to walk away from a hard-fought negotiation. It is tough to invest a lot of time only to give up. The reason for this behavioral obstacle is called the *sunk cost fallacy*. This is a term in behavioral economics that says we become much more invested in completing a task once we have spent time working on it.

In the Big Dig tunnel project connecting the city of Boston to Logan Airport, the contractor was $5 billion over budget and still hadn't completed the job. During a meeting of the supervising committee, many lobbied against firing the contractor because of the enormous outlay they had already made. By the time the Big Dig was completed, it was years late and $15 billion over budget. But the worst part was on opening day. A loose tile fell down from the ceiling of the tunnel, shattering the windshield of a car and killing a family of four. While hindsight is always 20/20, a rational and logical person would have fired the contractor and put penalties in the new contract as well as performance bonuses.

During the Great Recession of 2008, President George W. Bush was faced with the bankruptcy of General Motors. GM was on the verge of bankruptcy, with a million workers at risk of losing their jobs. The US Treasury loaned $30 billion to GM in September 2008, hoping to save all those jobs.

When Barack Obama was elected president, he was still faced with the looming bankruptcy of GM. He instructed the treasury to give GM another $48 billion in May 2009, again to save more than a million jobs. In June 2009, GM officially went bankrupt. The US government gave GM more than $78 billion, only to see the company eventually fall into bankruptcy. For companies the size of GM, bankruptcy can take many shapes, from reorganization to a discharge of debt; it doesn't always mean liquidation. But the mistakes the US government made preceding GM's bankruptcy only wasted money.

This is a good example of the sunk cost fallacy. All the money that was put into GM made no difference; it entered bankruptcy anyway. Yet US Treasury dollars kept flowing in because money had already been committed. As a result, in 2009, every man, woman, and child in America was saddled with an extra $700 per person to pay for this mistake.

That's why it is so difficult to walk away from a negotiation. You have already invested your time, and sometimes your money. You start rationalizing that any deal is better than no deal at all.

Financial writers often say the average family buys a car every five years. By doing this, they will spend more than $800,000 on autos over their lifetime. Instead, I buy the nicest car I can think of and keep it for a decade.

When I bought my Porsche Cayenne S, the salesperson quoted $85,000 to take it home that day. But I was willing to walk away. I asked for his business card while he was talking to another couple. I wrote down "$69,000" with my cell phone number and a note that said, "Call me if you want to do this deal." My wife and I went to get sushi for lunch. I said, "If he doesn't call in the next twenty minutes, we will keep looking."

Surprisingly, the salesperson called in eighteen minutes and accepted our offer. I was in love with the car. I made $16,000 in a thirty-minute negotiation. But there was a problem with the salesperson accepting my offer so quickly. Can you imagine what it was? You got it! I might have gotten a better deal. Perhaps he would have accepted $65,000. I will never know.

Negotiation should be fun. It should be about reading the other side, communicating effectively, and using systematic tactics. It's like learning a new language. For the first few months, Spanish was pretty awkward for me, but as I practiced and got better, it became a lot more fun. If you practice these techniques, you will be more successful.

Most importantly, develop a negotiation mindset. When you start looking at everything as a potential negotiation, you will get very good at it and will have a lot more fun.

KEY TAKEAWAYS

1. Always be prepared to walk away.
2. The best negotiators walk away from ten deals for every one they accept.
3. Have fun when you negotiate. Treat it like language to be practiced and learned everyday.

Tactic 12: Take It or Leave It

This is one of most difficult statements to overcome. The *take it or leave it* demand make it seem as if you will either surrender or accept defeat.

This statement demands a yes or a walkaway. It is often used by poor leaders who are asked by subordinates for a raise, extra vacation time, or some other accommodation. The subordinate may say, "I've been here for a year. You said that I could get a pay increase after twelve months. What is the status of that?" The poor leader might say, "We don't have any more money in the budget for salaries this year. Take it or leave it."

In another example, you would love to try a new negotiation technique on a seller. Perhaps they are not the decision maker or have no interest in doing a deal. They say, "The price is what's on the sticker. Take it or leave it."

Whether you're negotiating a salary or a better deal on a product, there is a way to respond to this inartful phrase.

The answer is halfway between a joke and getting the other side to be more engaged. Here are a couple of tips you can use to get past this impasse:

Ask to speak to their supervisor. While this is typically a customer service demand, you can use this request here. You can say, "I know how difficult this must be for anyone in your position. Who might be authorized to make an exception to this rule?" Or "I'm sure some higher-up made these rules and didn't allow you to make exceptions. Would you mind if I had a short chat with that person? Can I have their name?"

Appeal to their sense of fairness. People are not robots. They realize when a rule or an instruction is unreasonable. If you treat people with respect and decency, they will often compromise to benefit you. You could say, "If I were to personally make it worth your while, is there something you could do?" A better and more direct way of asking this question is, "I know you are in a tough spot. But what would it take to make a small exception in this case?"

Government officials are the least likely to negotiate. No one has a take it or leave it attitude more than customs and immigration officials. In 1986, I flew to a convention speech in Tahiti with my then wife, Sandy. Arriving at Tahitian immigration, Sandy was flagged for an expired passport. These days, the gate agent at the departing city always verifies passports. If they make a mistake, the departing airline is required to fly the passenger back at the airline's expense. Normally this is a take it or leave it scenario—not even a choice. You are being deported. The French immigration officer told us he would send Sandy on the next flight to Los Angeles.

"I know how difficult this is for you," I said. "I completely respect the French laws here. But is there something we can do? A fine perhaps? Or something like a temporary visa that can be issued in this kind of case?"

The immigration officer jokingly said, "If I landed in Los Angeles with an expired passport, and you were the immigration officer, what would you do?"

I smiled and said, "If you arrived from Tahiti, you probably would want to go to Disneyland with your kids. I would never want to disappoint your kids by sending them back. I would issue a temporary ten-day visa at least to make your kids happy."

He smiled back at me, pulled out a stamp with something written in French and said, "You have ten days in my beautiful country. Stay any longer, and we will put you in jail." I thanked him and set the land speed record departing his office.

In a take it or leave it scenario, it's easy to think you have no options. But you always do—as long as there is someone to negotiate with. Remember you are communicating with a human being, not an algorithm.

There is a rule of thumb for a negotiation impasse: "When in doubt, ask questions." Whenever you get stuck or run out of options, ask questions. This may not produce a clear path to the outcome you want, but it will produce more options.

When most airline travelers are faced with a lengthy delays or cancellations, they immediately react with denial and anger at the gate agent announcing the bad news. But they should be asking when the next flight is, what other airlines providing service, or even when the arriving flight is scheduled.

There are a lot of take it or leave it scenarios that don't even catch your attention. Your home electricity is cut off because you forgot to make a payment. Your water is cut off because the payment is late. Your new home mortgage is delayed, potentially costing you thousands of dollars in extra penalties and relocation expenses.

These scenarios would probably cause you to become angry. Sometimes you might reach a customer service person who states the take it or leave it line. But now you know to stay calm and ask questions. As long as you have someone to talk to, you can find a way out. If you can't reach a human being, call again.

In the mid-1990s, I had another immigration scenario where I had the chance to use the take it or leave it strategy. Before NAFTA, anyone working in Canada for one month or one hour needed a work visa. Generally, my speeches were sixty to ninety minutes only. These visas were so cumbersome that it took months to get the Canadian government to respond. Most of my speeches were booked less than three months ahead. To avoid red tape, I took a shortcut and declared myself as a tourist.

I realized this was the wrong thing to do. I got caught in Edmonton trying to get through immigration. I was wearing a blue blazer and probably looked too professional to be a tourist. I was sent to a cubicle and waited three hours for an official to appear.

The officials found some audio programs in my suitcase and asked why I was in Canada. I immediately confessed that I was giving a speech the next day to 100 business owners; I was the keynote speaker for the conference. The immigration officer said that I had violated their laws by entering Canada without a work visa. He said he would look for the next flight back to the US and deport me. (I later learned that once a country deports, you are never allowed back. I do a lot of speeches in Canada, and I'm glad I didn't know this at the time.)

"Is there anything you can do to help?" I said.

"My hands are tied," he said. "There is nothing I can do."

"I know this is very difficult," I said. "I didn't realize the severity of the situation that I put myself into. I deeply apologize. But there are a few hundred influential business owners that have come from all over Alberta to hear me speak tomorrow. Are there any exceptions within your rules that would allow me to give this short speech? I want to avoid disappointing this big audience."

The official looked at his follow officer and whispered into his ear for a few minutes. He said, "There is one exception. If the speech is no more than one hour during lunch, no work visa is required."

I smiled and said, "That's me, that's me!"

The meeting planner was outside customs and had waited patiently for hours. I told him my time slot needed to be moved to noon. He was only too happy to avoid losing his keynote speaker.

If I can get past a take it or leave it situation with a government official who rarely makes exceptions, so can you. Be creative. Don't take no for an answer. Be polite and offer suggestions that will allow this person to make a concession while saving face.

KEY TAKEAWAYS

1. Ask to speak to the person's supervisor.
2. Appeal to their sense of fairness.
3. Always be polite and respectful, but very assertive.

Tactic 13: The Hot Potato

One challenge in nearly every negotiation is the hot potato. This used to be a popular kid's game. One child would take a hot potato directly out of the oven and toss to another. Refusing to hold the burning potato very long, they would in turn throw it to somebody else until it became cool enough to hold.

This concept is used frequently by negotiation parties today. They have a problem and want you to solve it. Then they reject every solution you come up with. Or they want you to solve their hot potato problem by making concessions.

It's a favorite tactic of negotiators to cause you to make concessions to their hot potato demands. For example, a buyer wants you to make a price concession because their credit card limit is not high enough to purchase your product.

One group said my speaking fee was not in their budget. Would I take less? They were passing me the hot potato, trying to get a concession. First, I said, "Who has the authority to exceed the budget?" When that didn't work, I asked about their training budget. The meeting planner said the training department wasn't involved in the conference. I then offered to sell them a copy of my latest book for every attendee. Since educational material is part of training, I asked if that could be paid out of their training budget. I decreased my speaking fee, but made more money overall from book sales. I did accept the hot potato challenge, but I asked them for options instead of making concessions.

One Realtor heard a buyer would have to pay a higher interest rate for a mortgage than planned. The buyer wanted the seller to take back financing, making it the seller's problem instead of the buyer's. The selling Realtor did not accept the hot potato. Instead, she referred the buyer to a more aggressive mortgage broker specializing in hard money loans.

Never allow the other side to make their issue your problem. This will only create more concessions from you and produce a bad deal. My wife loves to tell her daughters, "Your lack of planning does not constitute my emergency." When my daughters put themselves into a crisis because they didn't plan ahead, we try to let them live with it. Perhaps they will plan better the next time.

One of my tennis friends was a new financial planner at Fisher Investments. I coached him for a few months, and he was doing great. I got a referral to his marketing VP for a possible speech. The VP passed me the hot potato by saying, "When you have made Alan the top producer in our company, we will consider you as a speaker." I responded to this arrogant VP by saying, "How much will your producers lose by not employing the skills that Alan is learning right now? If you want to wait and find out, I totally understand. But I am also working with your competitors."

The way to deal with the hot potato is to ask the other party to solve it. Simply say, "That sounds difficult. What do you think you should do?" Or you could say, "This seems like a tough situation. It would be a shame if we couldn't do this deal just because of that issue. How do you think you might solve that?"

In buying our cottage in Portugal, we asked the sellers if they were willing to leave the furniture. Since they lived in England, this seemed convenient, since they would either throw it away or haul it back at great expense. The sellers wanted an extraordinary amount for the furniture: $35,000. In Portugal, any sale incurs a 23 percent tax. The seller could increase the sales price of the house by $35,000 to allow them to pay a lower 15 percent capital gains tax. But this would only raise my own tax by $35,000 when I sold the property later.

I said to the sellers, "I'm not willing to increase my own tax by purchasing inexpensive furniture in the cottage. What do you think you should do?" I threw the hot potato back at them. We ended up settling on a very small amount of money outside of the home purchase price to buy the furniture.

It's important never to take responsibility for the other party's issue. Do not let them transfer the hot potato to you. Keep asking them how they will solve the problem. Of course, if they keep asking you to make concessions because of their hot potato, you have to be willing to walk away.

KEY TAKEAWAYS

1. Never let the other party's problem become your issue.
2. Don't make concessions to resolve the other side's challenges.
3. Ask how they plan to resolve their problems. Then suggest solutions they could implement.

3

Advanced Negotiation Techniques

Many negotiation books cover techniques and skills to achieve the outcome you want. Many discuss hard-core aspects of the subject such as buying, selling, and even salary negotiations. But there are other questions as well. For example, can you be too enthusiastic to buy or sell? Does an adversarial attitude create entrenched attitudes and make each party more difficult to negotiate with? Can you negotiate with a committee? Can you use negotiation techniques to communicate with those who have customer complaints?

Many books also discuss how to win a negotiation, but very few talk about how to listen the other side into accepting your ideas. Listening is different from persuading. The listener always controls the conversation. The better you listen, the less you will have to persuade.

When you present solutions to reach a successful negotiated outcome, you may get objections. These are only requests for more information. They do not signal the end of the negotiation—only that the other side has concerns to overcome.

This chapter will cover all these areas and make your next negotiation even easier, with more successful results.

Technique 1: How to Handle Tough Negotiations

PRICE, TIMING, AND QUALITY

In 1982, I learned as a new business speaker that there are three things negotiators want in every deal but never completely attain: *price*, *timing*, and *quality*. We all want to get the best price possible. We also want it now. We want the quality to be the best. But we can only get two of these three things: You can get a great price right now, but it won't be the best quality. You can get a product with great quality now, but you will pay a lot. You can get both great price and great quality, but you will have to wait.

You will never get all three. If you think that you will get a great price, immediate timing, and the best quality, you will lose the negotiation, because the other side will see your weakness and gain concessions from you.

I'm a pretty good travel planner, but sometimes I miss the timing windows for the best deals. I've been flying for forty years and know the best prices are booked between three and five weeks before departure. But sometimes I get busy and forget to secure the reservation.

This happened about a year ago. I remembered a week before a speech that I had forgotten to make an airline reservation. A last-minute round-trip ticket to Houston with American, United, or Delta cost more than $1,000. I had promised my client that the airfare would be no more than $750. I would either have to eat the $250 or fly on a discount airline. This was the first time I ever flew Spirit, which, I learned, is the worst airline in America. Spirit is so cheap that they charge for emotional baggage.

I booked a ticket for $500 and paid an extra $250 to check two bags for a center seat in coach. The ticket agents and flight attendants acted as if the passengers were enemies.

This is an example of getting price and timing, but not quality. Always be ready in any negotiation to get the two most important. But remember that you will never get all three.

THE RELUCTANT BUYER

One of most effective negotiation strategies you can ever use is reluctance. Negotiators who seem desperate nearly always get a bad deal. Buyers and sellers who can take it or leave it seem more often to get what they want. The weaker side of a negotiation always makes the most concessions. Never let the other side know the pressure you are under. You should never expect concessions without also giving something up in return.

Let's talk about how you can apply the reluctant buyer strategy. Suppose you want to buy a car from a private party—a five-year-old Porsche in perfect condition. The color is gorgeous. The convertible top is in great shape and actually matches the body. The owner lets you take a test drive. The rush of the acceleration excites you.

You know this is the one. Do you display your enthusiasm and tell the owner how much you want it? This is a good idea if you want the seller to suspect that his price is too low; perhaps he should just raise it.

Or should you take a walk around the car emotionlessly? After the test drive, you tell the owner, "I guess it's OK." You indicate that you've seen a few of these cars, and you may just keep looking. Being a master negotiator, you try to get the seller to discount his price even before you've made an offer. You might say, "I know you want $50,000 for this car. I've seen a few others that are pretty good. What's the lowest price you would take for it?" If you're lucky, the seller might immediately discount to $45,000. You can then bracket the price you want. If you are unlucky, the seller might stick with $50,000, but you have still softened them up. If you want to pay $47,000, you would offer $44,000, waiting for the seller to counter. And at $50,000, the car is still a good buy. Perhaps they will throw in a car cover or buy the first year of an extended warranty. None of this will be possible unless you act reluctant.

THE RELUCTANT SELLER

You can use the same strategy on the other end, applying the reluctant seller. You want to sell a Porsche for $50,000. The buyer takes a walk around the car, showing their enthusiasm; after all, it's difficult to find a Porsche in such good shape. They take it for a test drive. You can see the joy on their face. The buyer says, "What's the lowest you would take for this car?" You then tell the buyer that you love the car; it's really difficult to sell it; you don't even know why you put up for sale. Probably the right thing to do is to give it to your kids and keep it in the family. You then look at the buyer and ask, "What was that again? I didn't quite hear what you just said." The buyer retracts his request and says, "Would you rather have a cashier's check, or shall I wire the money to you?"

In Donald Trump's *The Art of the Deal*, he describes a negotiation for the St. Moritz Hotel in New York City. The Australian real estate developer Alan Bond wanted to buy the hotel and met with Trump directly. He walked into Trump's office asking how much he wanted for the St. Moritz.

Trump used the reluctant seller technique to maximize his price. He said, "Alan, I'm so sorry you came all the way down here for the St. Moritz. It isn't for sale. But I have another property on the West Side that I would love to discuss."

Bond said, "This is outrageous. Your staff said that we could meet about the St. Moritz, and now you're saying it's not for sale. I flew twenty hours from Australia for nothing."

Trump stood up and walked Bond to the elevator, saying, "I'm so sorry for the miscommunication, Alan." As he pushed the down button for the elevator, he said, "Alan, I deeply apologize. But if you did want to make an offer for the St. Moritz, how much would you pay?"

From this very simple tactic of getting Bond to make the first offer, Trump was able to bracket Bond's offer. In the end he sold the property for $160 million, netting him $81 million in profit. Trump made tens of millions in one hour because he was an effective negotiator.

Technique 2: Avoiding Confrontation in Negotiation

Negotiation is about getting to yes. But yes is also about making sure both sides win. When a negotiation does not go well, one side may get emotional. It's up to you to avoid confrontation and defuse tension.

I'm a member of the Daniel Island Club in Charleston, South Carolina. It is a private golf community, with 700 members and homeowners in a very enclosed environment. It has an impressive tennis complex, a pickleball facility, a world-class gym, and impressive dining facilities.

When I first arrived here in April 2021, I was blown away by the stellar customer service displayed by everybody who worked here. I asked one server if they held classes on being nice to the members. She simply said, "We don't have classes, but we do have a culture of saying yes."

It would be easy to take this welcoming policy for granted, but every member knows to value and respect the people that work here. In other words, we make sure we always preserve this wonderfully friendly culture.

The same is true in a negotiation. There are some who can get results negotiating from a position of power and arrogance. But you will get far better results negotiating with a mindset of respect, empathy, and politeness.

In almost every cop show, you see an interrogator threatening a suspect with a life in jail or the death penalty. In reality it's almost always the opposite. A Dallas police interrogator heard me speak recently. We chatted over a cup of coffee after my speech. He told me that even when suspects lie, the interrogator tries to show empathy.

One suspect, accused of burglary, denied everything. The interrogator knew from the victim's statement that the perpetrator had broken and entered the house trying to recover his watch (just like O.J. Simpson trying to recover sports memorabilia). The Dallas cop said, "Sometimes people enter a house trying to recover something that was stolen from them. I can just imagine what it's like knowing that an object of great importance to you was taken. There's nothing you can do to get it back. That is really disgusting. I wouldn't even put up with it."

The suspect then chimed in, "That's exactly what happened to me. I just wanted my watch back, and there was nothing else I could do."

The cop said, "Tell me exactly what happened, and I'll try to help you." The suspect was drawn into negotiating with the interrogator, whose goal was to get the suspect to confess. This too is a form of negotiation.

To avoid confrontation, first, never argue. Never try to put the other side down or accuse the other side of bad intentions. This happens in politics all the time. One side tries to demonize the other to whip up their own base. It only causes the other side to solidify their stand.

FEEL, FELT, FOUND

Another technique that works very well in keeping the other side from feeling confronted is called *feel, felt, found*: "I understand how you feel. I have felt the same as you in the past. But if we can reach an agreement on this, I think we both look back at this with pride that we were able to resolve everything."

One of the most painful negotiations is divorce. A speaker friend's ex-wife threatened to take away his business, impose huge alimony payments, take all his copyrights, and limit time seeing his daughter. He would have accepted all of her demands except for having time with his daughter taken away. The ex-wife constantly berated him, accusing him of being a bad husband and a bad father. He was unable to negotiate and ended up in a two-week court battle to gain time with his daughter, which cost $200,000 in legal fees. Most of both sides' assets were wiped out.

My friend would have accepted the initial offer if the wife had not attacked. Confrontation never works in a negotiation. If you become angry, it will only become your expensive personal emotional catharsis. It is much better to stay calm and walk away if the negotiation gets too heated. You can always reengage later. Don't burn any bridges.

SUBJECT TO

Have you ever been involved in a negotiation that wasn't moving quickly enough? The answer to getting through an impasse is called *subject to*.

The subject to can be used in many types of negotiations. One of my coaching clients was unable to sign a contract because he had ongoing financial commitments for the next three months. I knew that revisiting coaching too distant in the future would kill the deal, so I did a subject to. I said, "As long as your goal is to double your business next year, let's get the agreement signed and start coaching in January. If you need to delay until February or March, that's fine too. Does that work for you?"

If you ever suggest a subject to and the other side won't agree, be prepared to walk away. Interested negotiators find a way to reach an agreement. Uninterested negotiators stall and waste your time.

A car dealer recently told me that subject to is used every day in their dealership. An interested couple can't make a decision until they qualify for financing. An inexperienced salesperson will let them go home, promising the finance manager will call later. An experienced sales rep will write the deal up on the spot subject to financing. They will get all the paperwork done and then walk in the finance manager's office. Even if they find out the interest rate is higher than expected, the momentum will motivate the sides to complete the negotiation.

The subject to is effective everywhere, in any industry. A loan officer wants to get paperwork started with a home buyer who is still looking. They suggest getting prequalified so they know how much house they can buy.

A landscaper negotiates with a homeowner who wants to redo the hardscape around a newly purchased property. The owner doesn't want to sign a contract until they can settle on a landscape plan. The landscaper suggests signing a contract subject to the owner agreeing to the hardscape plan they like. But in a more sophisticated, foot in the door twist, the landscaper also asks if they can start monthly maintenance so the foliage around the house doesn't get overgrown. By using a subject to, as well as a rejection then retreat tactic, the chances of a successful negotiation go up dramatically.

Recently a meeting planner didn't want to move ahead with booking me as a speaker until she secured the venue. She was unsure which day I would speak within a three-day block. She didn't want to sign the contract until the schedule was complete. I wanted to get the ball rolling and said, "Let's just book the program, subject to getting a meeting date." She asked what that meant. I said, "I will send you an agreement with a speaking fee, the topic, subject to you finalizing the meeting date. You just let me know when that date is, and we can fill it in later." This bridged the impasse. Doing a subject to is a wonderful technique for maintaining momentum. Usually it's harder to stop a rolling ball than get one started.

Subject to is often used in real estate. Perhaps the buyer wants to remodel a kitchen, but doesn't know the costs. Maybe the seller doesn't know how much they'll have to pay in capital gains tax, and doesn't want to make a decision until they find out. You can use a subject to by saying, "Let's confirm this offer, subject to your agreement to the kitchen remodel cost. Let's write this up subject to the capital gains cost." It will be much more difficult for the buyer or seller to stop the process to get all the information. Then restart it again.

Technique 3: Resort to a Committee
DON'T NEGOTIATE WITH THOSE WHO CAN'T SAY YES

Don't ever negotiate with someone who can't buy. Some of most difficult people to negotiate with are those who don't have the power to make a decision.

A key problem in negotiating is trying to get a better deal from somebody who can't give you any deal at all. It's always amazing to me to hear people ask front-line workers for discounts. A restaurant customer might ask for an extra drink from a server, who needs to check with a manager. An airline passenger asks a ticket agent to waive a ticket charge. The car repair customer asks for a discount from a service clerk. In all these cases, the worker will either ask the manager for direction or will inform the customer there are no discounts or exceptions.

Managers and owners are paid to generate initial and recurrent business. They know the value of making a customer happy. Front-facing workers focus on doing a job and often care only about their hourly paycheck. It's rare that anyone besides a manager will be interested in any request beyond their current duties. In a restaurant recently, a young food runner gave my wife lunch with a bagel instead of a brioche bun to go with her bacon and egg sandwich. Merita told the server she thought the lunch included the brioche bun. The food runner simply nodded and left. A manager would have immediately replaced the meal. The young food runner only cared about getting off work.

A few years ago, I got a great referral to three Canadian companies who might be able to use my services as a speaker. The referral source heard me at a conference and said to use his name. I asked to speak to the referred lead VP of sales and left a voicemail. An assistant called back and asked about my topics and speaking fees. I don't negotiate with someone who can't buy. I gave her the topics but said I would love to speak to the VP when he has time. She insisted on my fee one more time. I restated that I didn't know what the fee was until I found out more about their goals. After four decades as a speaker, I knew that she would present the topics and my fee to someone who had no idea who I was. It would have been a total waste of time. Don't sell or negotiate with someone who can't buy.

At one point I was a member of eSpeakers, a listing company for professional speakers. A few days before canceling my listing, a request popped up from a company in Northern California asking for my speaking fee. I responded with an email requesting a quick phone call. The response again asked only for my speaking fee. I again requested a phone call because I wanted to find out more about the meeting and the company before I quoted a fee. On the third response, the respondent wrote that he was new and was only shopping prices. They were yet ready to book anybody.

Once again, the rule holds. Don't sell or negotiate with someone who can't buy.

This is one of most difficult barriers you face in negotiating a deal. When you receive a call from someone who asks your price, add value before you quote a fee. Simply say, "There are a range of prices. I would like to find out more about you and your needs before we discuss them. Is that OK with you?" Anyone who insists on a price before finding out the value is unlikely to be a qualified buyer.

There are exceptions. If your product or service is small, you may not have time to go through this process. But when you offer something that is competitive and isn't a commodity, find out more before disclosing a price. You are in essence making the first offer.

But first, always ask about their position. A useful question is, "Are you the person making the final decision, or is there somebody else you need to get approval from?" Generally, you will get a name. Make sure that person is in attendance when you make a presentation.

WHEN THE DECISION MAKER IS A COMMITTEE

Often a committee is making a decision, with an assistant collecting information. When you find this out, always ask for the name of the committee chair. Then ask the assistant if you can talk directly to that person. This generally works, because the assistant is unlikely to have ever been asked that in the past. Sometimes they will ask the committee chair for permission first.

Equally bad is negotiating with somebody who believes you are the only decision maker. This will take away some of your options. Don't forget: those with the most options have the most power. It's often good to say you need to check with someone else. It is equally important to take away their higher authority. In other words, retain yours, but remove theirs.

I've only missed three speeches in forty years. When I was flying into Las Vegas for one presentation, thunderstorms in Chicago were prohibiting any flights from taking off or landing. I kept in contact with the meeting planner in Las Vegas. By the time I realized my flight would not arrive until three hours after the scheduled speech, the meeting planner and I agreed there was no point in my still attempting to arrive in Las Vegas.

The next week I spoke to the meeting planner and the president of the association by phone. I agreed to refund the speaking fee and absorb the airfare. But the meeting planner became irrational. She wanted me to pay for all the audiovisual expenses as well. While damages weren't in my contract, I knew that saying no abruptly would simply exacerbate an already difficult situation. So I reverted to a higher authority. I said, "I will have to check with my partner and get back to you." My partner back in those days was my wife. While she was sure to listen, her opinion had no bearing. This tactic was enough to cool down the situation. The meeting planner and the president eventually just let it go.

Again, if you can, it's a great idea to refer to your higher authority but take away theirs. Your higher authority can be your wife, friend, or an advisor. This is a tool you should always keep in your tool chest to get a better deal.

Technique 4: How to Negotiate Complaints

Skillful negotiation tactics can be used to gain concessions besides money. You can apply them in many areas of your life, for example dealing with upset customers or resolving conflict.

An upset customer calls. Most would probably just walk away and never use your product or services in the future. You may not even know why. But ignorance is not bliss. The lifetime value of a customer isn't limited to a single transaction; it lasts throughout the relationship over many years. Any good, frequent customer is a huge benefit. They're willing to tell you what they don't like. You should be able to make changes to prevent dissatisfaction in the future.

Sometimes a customer or client can be unreasonable and may want to call just to complain about irrational things. You should respond in the same way as if you were dealing with a customer with a valid complaint or one who is just high-maintenance.

Here's how the conversation might go. The customer calls and says how upset they are. You listen and possibly push back. You let them know how good the product or service is and how few people have problems. This makes the customer even more upset, since their complaint was not taken seriously. Even if you've offered a concession, at this point the customer is upset and won't listen to anything else you say. At this point the conversation goes off the rails, and the customer hangs up.

As we've discussed, the customer will tell three people about a great experience (but only if it's exceptional). Unsatisfied customers will tell twelve people about their bad experience. On social media, an irate customer may be able to let hundreds or thousands know about it. It would be much better to create a happy customer in spite of any issues they may have had.

THE FOUR STEPS TO A HAPPY CUSTOMER

The four steps for creating a happy customer are:

1. Listen.
2. Ask what they would like you to do.
3. Negotiate the solution.
4. Trial close.

Let's take the steps one by one.

1. **Listen.** Ask the customer's name and how you can help. Don't be defensive. Especially don't diminish the customer's emotions. If you have ever felt your emotions were disregarded, you can imagine how a customer would feel. At this point, only show empathy. Make comments such as, "I'm sorry that happened." Or, "That must have been very difficult for you." It doesn't matter which empathic phrases you use; make people feel understood.

   In one US Trust study, 83 percent of respondents bought because they felt understood. Only 6 percent purchased because they were made to understand. Especially during a customer complaint, you will not be able to reason or persuade them otherwise. Don't try.

2. **Ask what they would like you to do.** Every upset customer feels they have to prove fault to get restitution. Sometimes they are truthful, but often they fabricate the details. In any case, they are emotional. They don't expect you to ask how you can resolve the issue at the very beginning of the conversation. They are prepared to make an extensive case. They're not prepared for agreement so quickly. Think about this: You are not suggesting they get anything they want. You're only trying to get them to make the first offer. Most of the time, their request is much less than you would be willing to settle for.

3. **Negotiate the solution.** The upset customer has made the first offer. Now use your skills to reach a compromise. If what the customer wants is far less than you are willing to give, just say yes. This usually works. Sometimes they are only asking for an apology. Other times, they only want a replacement.

   If you have to negotiate, just say, "I don't think I can . . . but if we could . . . would that be OK?" The customer expects you to defensively push back. They will be so surprised at your consideration that their emotions will be immediately diffused.

4. **Trial close.** It's important to get agreement before you finalize any negotiation. The customer wants you to do one thing. You've made an offer to do something less. Possibly they've agreed, but you still have to ask for their agreement and commitment to the solution. For example, if you agree to send them a replacement product and pay for the shipping costs, ask, would they be happy?

   A trial close is gaining commitment and buy-in to a negotiation. Various trial closes could be, "If we could . . . would that be OK?" Or, "If I could arrange with my manager to get you X, would that be a good resolution for you?" If you need to negotiate, it may be a good idea to mention a higher authority and then trial-close. Even if you are sure your manager will accept it, it's still important to trial-close.

   Recently I went to my bank in person with a complaint about an overdraft fee that I felt was in error. There were no managers in the office, so I told the teller what happened. She said there was nothing she could do; I should contact the main office. I became irritated with the lack of resolution and told her just to close my account.

Just then a manager came around the corner and asked me what happened. I told him that I was irritated and should never been charged the $36 overdraft fee. I expected to argue with him, but he used the steps outlined above to resolve complaints. He apologized for the fee and said it must have been an error in their system. He asked me what I would like him to do. I said, "Just reverse the $36." He then trial-closed by saying, "I will take a look at the account. If I can reverse it, would you be OK with that?"

I said, "Sure," and checked my account the next day. The manager did what he told me he would do, and he kept a customer. The fact that I'm writing about this experience indicates what a good job he did.

According to Harvard Business School studies, a happy customer is 36 percent more likely to be loyal, but an unhappy customer who has an issue successfully resolved is 83 percent more likely to be loyal. Customers will be more loyal as a result of a successful resolution than if they had never had a problem at all.

Here's another example using the four steps.

UPSET CUSTOMER: I just received a golf club in the mail from your company, and the grip is damaged.
SERVICE REP: I'm sorry to hear that.

UPSET CUSTOMER: I'm really tired of getting damaged goods in the mail. I waited too long for this and wanted to play golf this week. Now I can't even use the wedge I bought for a tournament I'm playing in on Friday.

SERVICE REP: I'm sorry the grip is damaged. What would you like me to do?

UPSET CUSTOMER: I just want a wedge that is undamaged. It would be nice if I can get it by Thursday so I can play in the tournament.

SERVICE REP: Let me check with my manager. But if I can arrange it to be delivered by Thursday, would that be helpful?

UPSET CUSTOMER: That would be great; thank you.

SERVICE REP: I've just checked with my manager, and we will send it out today. It should be there by Thursday, so you can play in the tournament. All we need is to get the damaged club back in ten days, so we don't have to charge you for two clubs. Is that OK?

UPSET CUSTOMER: Absolutely. Thank you so much for helping.

Think of how seamless this interaction was. The service rep was immediately empathetic and asked what the customer would like him to do. He offered to talk to the manager but trial-closed first to make sure the customer would be happy with the solution. The customer was happy, because he was able to use the new club in a tournament. Everything worked out well. Now the upset customer is 83 percent more likely to do business in the future with that company, simply because they had an issue that was successfully resolved.

This is just one way of using negotiation techniques in a way you may not have thought of. You can use it to resolve customer complaints, buy and sell, and even negotiate conflict with your spouse or friends. All you have to do is practice. Reading this book alone will not help you. You have to take these ideas and implement them immediately.

Technique 5: Probing for Needs

One aspect of negotiation even experts miss is how to listen to the other side. After all, negotiation is really the process of building a relationship while making a deal. You are not reaching an agreement with a robot. You are dealing with people possessing biases, worries, dreams, and goals, just like you.

Research at the University of California at San Diego showed that trust is worth 17 percent of the gross price of a product or service. In a sales setting, if you have trust, you can increase your prices by 16 percent and still not lose a client. Without trust, a client or customer would leave you for a mere 1 percent discount offered by a competitor. This is critical during a negotiation, because trust can not only help you get a better deal, but can pave the way for future deals.

Effective probing is critical in gaining trust. The more rapport you have, the more trust you will gain. The more you probe, the less you have to close. The more you listen to needs, the less you have to persuade. Probing is everything.

Probing is listening intently to what other people want. It is the way to dovetail your needs to the other party's. If you can probe effectively, you can do any deal with anybody at any time.

Let's assume you want to get a great deal on a new Porsche Carrera. Most dealers don't make deals on these popular cars. They'd much rather sell you a Porsche Cayenne. Normal negotiation strategies suggest first finding out the dealer's invoice price, then make an offer they will accept. But if you're good at probing, you will first ask about how many Carreras are currently in inventory. You would find out which car has been on the lot longest. You would try to find out the salesperson's biggest concerns—hopefully the one most likely to motivate them to make a deal.

For example, is the 4S model less popular than the turbo? Is the S model more popular than the standard Carrera? After all these questions, you might ask how much pressure the salesperson is under at the end of the month to hit their quotas. When you learn all these things, you can come back at the end of the month and get a better deal on the less popular model or color that they are trying to move.

All this comes from probing effectively. Prescription without diagnosis is malpractice. A way to find out what the other side wants is to use a technique called the *five-step bridge*. This is a way to sell without selling, to close without closing, negotiate without negotiating. It's a way to find out what people want and then giving it to them.

THE FIVE STEP BRIDGE

1. Introduction.
2. Search for needs.
3. Recap.
4. Trial close.
5. Present a solution.

1. **Introduction**. This first step is breaking the ice by asking a question. It's a way of engaging in the first few minutes by finding out more about the person you could be negotiating with. For example, let's assume that you want to negotiate an apartment lease. The first thing you would do is let the owner know how beautiful and well-maintained you think the complex is. You might also praise the floor plan.

   But then you should start asking questions about how many units are there, how full the complex is, and the types of tenants the owner likes to rent to. While many of these questions are standard, any information will help you meet the needs of the owner. When the owner benefits, you will also. You will get a better deal.

2. **Search for needs** (get three). According to US Trust, one need presents a 36 percent chance of doing a deal. Two needs equal a 53 percent chance, and three needs would give you a 93 percent chance of making a deal happen. So if you can uncover three needs on the other side, you will gain more concessions and help the negotiation move more quickly.

   The same research showed that if a bank or other vendor has one product with you, there is a 36 percent chance of retaining your business over five years. Two products will give the bank a 53 percent chance of keeping your business. Three products will give them a 93 percent chance of keeping you as a customer for more than five years.

   The concept of three is very important. People can only remember and retain around three things in memory. We forget 70 percent of what we see, hear, and feel within twenty-four hours. We forget 90 percent after three days. Memory is limited and fleeting. It is very important to keep needs and concepts limited to three.

During seminars, I prove this point by reading ten two-digit numbers to the audience. They are instructed not to write them down or record them in any way. At the end of reading the numbers, I ask all the attendees to read back from 100 out loud. At that point I ask one random audience member how many numbers they can remember. Most recall two; some will remember only one. In all my years of doing this exercise, nobody has ever remembered five.

If you can get three needs, not only will they be remembered, but you can use them to make the negotiation more relevant, persuasive, and concise. It will be challenging for you to listen to someone's emotions and create needs out of them. You can break down emotions by asking what they mean. For example, "I know you say it's frustrating; what do you mean by that?" A landlord might drill their answer down and say, "Frustrating means there a lot of people who can't afford this apartment. I wish I could screen them more effectively." So one need would be for a tenant to relieve the owner's frustration by being able to afford the lease.

3. **Recap.** Eighty-three percent of people buy because they feel understood. Only 6 percent do business because they are made to understand. The recap does all this. Every good psychotherapist will listen and repeat what a client says; the best therapists

use the client's exact words. For example, they will say, "If I heard you correctly, you are frustrated with your kids' lack of respect. Did I get that right?"

Our way of using this in negotiation is to say, "If I heard you correctly, you are frustrated because the prospective tenants often can't afford the rent. Also, it's too time-consuming to show the property to unqualified people. And doing unnecessary credit checks are cumbersome. Did I get that right?"

By using the recap technique, you are making the other side feel understood. Negotiation is not only about getting the best price. It is also about solving problems. If you could find out what they are, you will get a better deal and develop a stronger relationship.

Think about how powerful this technique can be in your day-to-day relationships. What if your spouse is concerned about something? You listen for a few minutes and break those concerns down to three needs. Sometimes they need solutions. Other times your spouse simply needs to be listened to and shown empathy and sympathy. But if you recap what you heard back to them, they will feel understood and grateful that you could help guide them through that episode in their lives.

I jokingly tell my male clients that the five-step bridge is really a chick magnet. Many of my single female friends say men don't listen very well; they talk about themselves and don't really pay attention to the concerns of their dates. But the men who listen, gain three needs, and then recap what they heard become instantly more attractive. Some wives have even asked me to teach these techniques to their husbands. I always laugh, but it's pathetic that spouses don't listen using these skills.

4. **Trial close.** This step is the way to get the other side to commit to a solution before you present one. State the three needs, and ask if they are open to hearing about how to reach a solution. The important part is the elegance used in asking the question. For example, "If we could talk more about . . . would that be helpful?" Or you could say, "If we could talk more about how to make this process less frustrating, Ms. Apartment Owner, would that be beneficial?"

It's a way to get the other side to commit. It's also a way to find out if the needs are important. I played a doubles tennis match a few years ago. At the bar after the match, my partner said, "You are a business psychologist, right?"

"Yes, in fact I write books and speak around the world."

"I have a hammerhead salesperson who comes in late, leaves early, annoys my staff, and isn't even hitting his sales goals."

"Let me get this straight," I said. "You have a salesperson who comes in late, leaves early, annoys your staff, and isn't even achieving his goals. Did I get that right?"

"Absolutely."

I then trial-closed by saying, "If we could take a look at what to do about this guy, would that benefit you?"

He looked at me, and said, "Nope. I'm good. Beer?"

In other words, he didn't want to solve the problem; he just wanted to vent. Perhaps he just wanted me to listen and show empathy, which I did. I could have discussed how to do a three-step reprimand, how to behavior shape using praise, the critical path theory of management, and even how to motivate people to perform better. But since he was unwilling to commit to a solution, I just smiled and kept listening.

5. **Present a solution.** Once you find out needs, recap and trial-close, present a solution tailored to the other side. Limit your comments to addressing only their three needs. It will be very tempting to do an information dump of everything you know, but that will cause confusion. Confusion will create a desire for more information. When that happens, the other side will become paralyzed, not wanting to make a bad decision. They will walk away and do nothing.

   This is what you need to do in all of your negotiations. Listen for three needs, recap what you heard, and ask if the other side wants to work on a solution. We could call this *needs-based negotiation*, because you are not just negotiating a deal, you are building a relationship that may have a financial component to it.

Here's some homework for you. Try the five-step bridge on your spouse, kids, or friends. Try to uncover three needs, then recap, and then trial-close. The real trick is making it elegant. This is one of the most important communication skills you will ever learn in sales, management, or any form of negotiation.

DISCOVERING DECISION STRATEGIES

Would be beneficial if you knew your negotiating partner's decision strategy? If you could figure out what the other side is likely to offer or counteroffer, would your negotiation go more smoothly and possibly become more lucrative?

THE INSTANT REPLAY TECHNIQUE

The answer lies in past behavior. I call it *instant replay*. The underlying concept is based on the notion that people don't change. How people behaved in the past indicates how they will behave in the future. This idea probably makes intuitive sense to you. In fact, the great developmental psychologist Jean Piaget concluded that adult personalities are set in concrete between the age of two and seven years old. We can learn skills after seven, moderate behavior, and even become more disciplined. But the basic core of our personality is intact by the age of seven.

As proof, the divorce rate in America is about 62 percent for first marriages within ten years. Do you know the divorce rate for second marriages within ten years? It's a lot higher: second marriages end in divorce 78 percent of the time. I jokingly say the reason is that you took yourself with you to the second marriage—that is, the person you were in the first marriage is the same as the second. There are other factors. Teenage girls tend to resent the stepparent, especially if the biological parent does not support their spouse over their children. But by and large, the behaviors that created trouble in the first marriage will likely be the same in the second.

Alcoholics who stop drinking call themselves *recovering*, not *recovered*. They realize addiction is the real issue and is a deep part of their personality. They can cope, but they can't change who they are.

It's like the parable of the scorpion asking the frog to carry him across a pond. The frog said, "I won't do it. If I carry you, you will sting me, and I will drown."

The scorpion said, "Why would I do that and drown us both?"

The frog agreed. The scorpion jumped on the frog's back. Midway through the trip, the scorpion stung the frog. Drowning, the frog said, "Look, now you've drowned us both." The scorpion replied, "I can't change who I am; that's my nature."

If you can find out how the other side made past decisions, you can assume that they will replicate the process. For example, if you are dealing with a car buyer, you might ask how they decided to buy their last brand. Don't be confused when value is the answer. Just dig deeper, and ask more questions. Does value mean price? Does it mean extended warranty? Does it even mean model year?

On the other end, the buyer might ask the salesperson what process they used to sell their last one. It might not have been because of price. It might have been the warranty, the reviews, or even speed of delivery.

Let's say you are negotiating a hotel room. You might overtly ask how the manager makes decisions on offering discounts. Is it based on the number of nights? Is it more important to do a deal on a last-minute reservation?

In a real estate environment, you might ask the seller how they decided on the last buyer. It could have been the speed of the escrow. It could also have been whether the buyers would take care of the property. When someone sells a pet, those kinds of questions are paramount.

You can see that probing and listening are critical to getting the deal you want. Emotional intelligence is a skill that will make any negotiation more successful. It is defined by listening, probing, and understanding the other side. Peter, one of my clients, engaged in an emotional intelligence role-play with another participant. He asked, "Do you like this approach so far?"

The listener said, "I guess."

I asked Peter, "What do you think he meant by 'I guess'?"

Peter thought the other side had just agreed. I asked the listener what he meant. He said, "I heard what he said, but I didn't really agree with the approach." Until you can listen so well that you can read between the lines and ask cogent questions, negotiations will always be rocky.

THE "LET'S ASSUME" TECHNIQUE

One of the best ways to listening and get needs is to get the other side to tell what they want. The *"let's assume"* technique will help you discover exactly what the other side wants and how they will decide to reach agreement. This is a very sophisticated psychological tool that few negotiators know how to use. It works like this:

"Let's assume we reached agreement on this. What happened that let you know it was successful and you got exactly what you want?"

If you're dealing with a home seller, they may say, "The right price is important, but I really would love to get this closed within three weeks. We're moving out of state, and we've bought a house.

It would be nice if this was not a long process. We were married in this house, so selling it to a good family that will enjoy it as much as we have is important too."

Being an emotionally intelligent negotiator, you would ask, "What does the right price mean to you? Since you've already bought a house, where is it located? What does a good family mean to you?"

Because of the skills you have already learned, you would use the five-step bridge. You would recap these three needs. You would say, "If I heard you correctly, you said . . . Did I get that right?"

Since you now know how to trial-close, you would reach commitment by saying, "If we could focus on . . . what would be the right direction for you?"

Recently I was in a negotiation for a group of four speeches. Before we ever discussed price, I asked, "Let's assume the presentation is over. What happened that let you know all your objectives were achieved and you and I both had a great relationship through the process?"

The meeting planner said, "The attendees increased their closing ratio and managed their time more effectively, and the speaker did their research so well that the group thought they were part of the company."

I recapped these needs. Next, I trial-closed and said, "If we can accomplish these things, do you think the presentation would be a success?" The meeting planner was excited and said, "If you can do all that, you could charge pretty much whatever you want for the speech." She jokingly added, "But please keep your speaking fee reasonable."

Through the let's assume technique, I learned it was not only about price. In fact, there were details much more important than my speaking fee. When I got the planner to verbalize what she really wanted, price became less important. The negotiation became much easier.

Negotiation is not only about gambits, responses, and rules; it's about people, emotions, and empathy. Like all communication, you have to be somewhat of a psychologist to get the outcome you want.

I sometimes hear that these techniques are manipulative. But all communication and behavior-based skills can be manipulative. It depends on the intent of the person using them. If you want to manipulate the other side, you can use these skills maliciously. But here's the rub: most people are sensitive to manipulation. If you are trying to use these techniques unethically, you will make people suspicious and kill more good deals than you get. If you use these techniques in a sincere effort to understand others more effectively, you will find out the intent and motivation of the other side and help them accomplish their goals more effectively.

Technique 6: Handling Objections

Have you ever heard an objection you couldn't handle? Ever answered one objection, only to have it followed by another? Objections are always about details. Agreements are always about the big picture. Your goal is to keep the client thinking about the outcome, or what the product or service will do for them.

What is the opposite of love? It isn't hate; it's indifference! If someone hates you, they are still emotionally engaged, albeit in an aggressive way. Hate and love are both sides of an emotional coin. But when people won't talk or ignore you, the relationship is done.

We *want* objections. We want people to tell us what they don't like as well as what they do like. Objections are just requests for more information. If they are talking, you are still in the game. When they stop talking, you are done. I jokingly say during speeches that when your spouse is ranting, raving, and upset, they are merely showing their emotion. But when they aren't talking to you, they are talking to their lawyer instead. Objections are always about worries that you or the product or service won't work or isn't the best deal for the client. All objections stem from too little trust.

HIGHER AUTHORITY

If someone appeals to a higher authority, it could mean that you aren't negotiating with the right person. One of the fastest ways to get an objection is to ask for a concession from somebody who can't say yes. Get the decision maker in the process as soon as you can. This is fundamental to creating a successful negotiation.

If you negotiate with the wrong person, they are likely to say, "I need to check with my boss." Or worse yet, they may say no without a reason. This is why it's important to ask questions and probe before you ask for any concessions.

Another objection based on higher authority is, "I will have to ask my partner." Or, "I have to check with my committee." We have earlier covered how to get through the higher authority response.

YOU HAVEN'T PROBED WELL ENOUGH

Most of the time negotiations fall apart because of lack of information. One side doesn't know the needs of the other. The reason is a lack of listening and probing. Listening poorly may work for minor negotiations, such as a small retail purchase. But when you negotiate for a car, computer system, or a real estate purchase, you'd better have a really good idea of what the other side needs and wants.

One of the best business communication thinkers of the last fifty years was J. Douglas Edwards. His teachings were always about asking questions to make each side aware of what the other wanted.

J. Douglas was on Mike Douglas's talk show in the late 1960s. Mike Douglas preceded Oprah Winfrey and Jerry Springer by several decades. The show set had daisies on the walls and looked like a typical 1960s stage. Mike Douglas was a chain smoker and displayed a big ashtray in the middle of the desk separating him from the guest.

When J. Douglas was introduced and the audience applauded, Mike invited him to sit at the table. Mike said, "I hear you are about the best business negotiator in the world."

J. Douglas said, "That's very kind; thank you."

Mike said, "Why don't you sell me this ashtray?"

J. Douglas said, "The one right there?"

"Yes. You have seven minutes before the next commercial break."

J. Douglas said, "What do you like about the ashtray, Mike?"

"I love the heft. It's a good paperweight for the notes I read during the commercial breaks. Otherwise the papers fly away when the swamp coolers come on."

"What else do you like about the ashtray?"

Mike said, "I like the channels on top. I want my cigarette to stay put and not fall off onto the desk. I'm afraid it'd burn the place down."

"What else do you like about the ashtray, Mike?"

"Well, it's green—my favorite color."

J. Douglas finally said, "How much would you pay for that ashtray, Mike?"

"I don't know. Five dollars, six dollars?"

J. Douglas said, "Sold; it's yours."

Isn't this the way every negotiation should progress? The first step is to find out more about the other side. Discover their goals and needs. Find out what they really want, and help them succeed at getting it. Negotiation is not a zero-sum game. It's not about you winning and them losing. It's about listening, probing, gaining trust, and finally reaching an outcome that benefits you both.

HOSTAGE RESCUE

A lot has been written about hostage rescue negotiation tactics. Most of these scenarios start with kidnapper making the first offer—the demand. The rescue negotiator then asks questions about the hostage taker's goals, concerns, frustrations, anxieties, and eventually outcomes. A successful negotiation involves listening and probing for psychological anxieties and needs. That's why psychologists often make the best negotiators. They are trained to listen for subtext and emotion beneath the words. If the FBI can keep the kidnapper focused on psychological solutions and how to get out of psychological pain, the negotiation often ends well.

A more difficult scenario is the professional kidnapping for ransom—especially international abductions. We see these in movies. The kidnappers abduct a loved one and make enormous financial demands. A good negotiator will make the perpetrator believe that the ransom may be reasonable, but they need more information.

The negotiator will find out about the kidnapper's organization, their goals, their view of injustice, and aggravations. The negotiator will never argue or allow the other side to produce objections. They will probe for needs while developing rapport and a level of trust in the process. Perhaps they can get the victim released or at least reduce the ransom price. In the end, a successful negotiation is built by listening and asking the right questions.

RISK AND REWARD ARE TOO CLOSE

Another reason for objections during a negotiation is the risk/reward ratio. You want to sell your '56 Chevy for $35,000. The other side can get it from a dealer for $37,000, and the dealer will throw in a one-year warranty. While the offers are close, the advantage goes to the dealer, who is offering a warranty. There is not enough difference in the deal to risk buying from a private party.

Another facet of the risk/reward objection is the benefit to the other side. Are you helping them achieve their goals also? Is there any benefit for them in the negotiation? Are you only asking for a price concession without the other side getting something in return?

HAVE YOU LOST RAPPORT?

Sometimes negotiations become difficult when one side is pushy or loses rapport. This is why people skills are so critical in building any good negotiated outcome.

In the Serengeti plain in Africa, Thomson's gazelle can run faster than any predator. Its antlers spiral up five to eight feet from its head. It is so fast that when chased by lions, hyenas, and leopards, it will jump nearly ten feet in the air, even though the jumps slow it down.

Gazelles can run 73 mph. The only animal that can take it down is the cheetah, which can run 75 mph in short bursts. The cheetah's strike range is about 200 yards. Sometimes cheetahs can get within 100 yards. The gazelles only look up to notice and then look back down to graze. Other times, when cheetahs get within 300 yards, the gazelles bolt. The difference is when their ears are down, they are hunting. And the gazelles know it.

If you become manipulative, forceful, or pushy, you will scare the gazelles away. Your negotiations will fail. It's critical to maintain rapport and control your emotions, even when the negotiation becomes stressful.

FEAR OF MAKING A CHANGE: STATUS QUO BIAS

Sometimes the other side of the negotiation is afraid of change. They are nervous about taking a risk. This is called *status quo bias*. It is displayed when one side prefers to negotiate with people they are already familiar with. Or the product or service may be unfamiliar. Perhaps it's a brand of golf clubs the customer has never used, or moving from an Android to an Apple iPhone. Even though Apple has a good reputation, the buyer has only had Android the last ten years.

These are all good examples of status quo bias, or a fear of making a change. Status quo bias will drive prices up for those influenced by it. If you want to buy a GM car and have owned GM for the last ten years, you will spend some $7,500 more because of your long experience. If you have owned Mercedes for the last ten years and want to buy the next new model, you will pay an average of $15,000 more for the privilege.

In one psychological study at the University of Chicago, students were asked to select one of four investments. One was a stock slightly less risky than the Standard & Poor's index. Another was a stock that was 20 percent more risky. A third choice was a municipal bond. The fourth choice was a regular bond, paying slightly more. All the students made choices. After deciding, they were informed they already owned one of the investments in their existing portfolio. Fifty-six percent of the students chose to stay with investment they had.

This is one reason many of us make bad choices when we negotiate. One of my coaching clients, Kathy, saw a seventy-five-year-old retiree who lost more than 35 percent of her retirement portfolio during the great recession of 2008. She had not seen her financial planner in ten years. Kathy took a look at the lady's portfolio and discovered it was much too risky for a woman of that age. Kathy rebalanced the retirement account, adding mostly safety, with a little growth. The retiree was so grateful that she told Kathy she would return the next day to sign all the documents to move the accounts.

The next day, the seventy-five-year-old retiree returned. Because of status quo bias, she called the broker she had not spoken to in ten years. He told her to keep money where it was. She told Kathy she would not be making any changes to her accounts. This is how status quo bias causes us to make bad decisions. We are so averse to making changes, even the most logical choices seem uncomfortable.

For someone younger, waiting for investments to return to previous levels would be a good idea. But when the retirement account is needed for income and has decreased, a loss in a portfolio may portend longevity risk. Or at some point, the retiree runs out of money and becomes totally dependent on Social Security.

NINE STEPS TO HANDLING TOUGH OBJECTIONS

Which of these problems do you experience the most? Do you get objections because you're too pushy? Do you negotiate with someone who can't say yes? Do you ask too few questions, so that you're unable to appropriately discover the other side's goals and decision strategies? Here are nine steps to handling any negotiation objection.

1. Uncover the real objection; don't let them stall.

When someone says they want to think about it, it is not an objection; it is only a stall. We have already discussed the problems created by a stall creates. When people say they want to think about it, it is often just another way of procrastinating. You will end up chasing them and wasting your time. They will walk out forgetting 70–90 percent of what was discussed and make no decision at all. Then you have to call a few times to reconnect.

The problem is that each time you reach out, it costs money. Each dial and message takes about ten minutes. If your time is valued at $100 an hour, this is like taking a $10 bill and tossing it in the trash every time someone wants to take time to think about it. Isn't a no better than wasting your time? Get the other side to give you a yes or no, but not a maybe. The up-front close is the answer.

Here is how to use the up-front close. To prevent the stall, you might say before the presentation, "If you decide this idea will work for you, I hope you will say yes. If there is any reason you don't like it, it's OK to say no. But I would like you *not* to say, 'Give me a few weeks; I'll get back to you later.' Because that tells me you don't have enough information to make an informed decision, and you won't hurt my feelings by saying no. Is that OK with you?"

Once you have presented your offer, you may still discover that the other side wants to talk before making a decision. This is where the Brueckner technique comes in. My client Tom Brueckner would present an offer but would leave the room before getting an answer. He would make his offer and say, "I need to sign a couple of documents. I will be right back. Can I get you a cup of coffee or more water?"

Tom will then walk over to the receptionist and chat about the weekend. After three minutes, he will walk back and ask, "Where are we at?" The brilliance of this strategy is it gives the other side a chance to think. It takes away the "I want to think about it" response.

There is also the *100/30 percent rule*. You can ask, "Do you want to make your decision based on 100 percent of the information or 30 percent? Because once you leave the room, you will forget 70 percent of all we talked about. Wouldn't it be better if we could talk right now, using 100 percent of the information?"

There is also the *up-front close reminder*. The last resort with the stall would be to remind the other party of their agreement to make a decision and ask, "Just out of curiosity, what is your biggest concern?" or "What worries you most?" If they don't know, suggest an objection. "Does the expense concern you?" The important thing is to get a real objection that you can talk about. If you let them stall you, the sale will usually not get done.

Here is an example of how this can go:

NEGOTIATOR 1: That's a great idea. I want to talk to my wife over the weekend and get back to you.

NEGOTIATOR 2: No problem. Take all the time you want. But last week, I mentioned that if we came up with a plan you didn't like, you'd tell me. If we came up with a plan that worked, you would tell me that also. So just out of curiosity, what is your biggest concern?

NEGOTIATOR 1: No concern. I just want to talk to my wife.

NEGOTIATOR 2: Is it the length of time? Is it tying your money up? Is it getting a better return somewhere else?

2. Hear them out.

Don't interrupt. One of the biggest mistakes negotiators make is believing they know what the other side is thinking. Often, they don't listen. They talk too much. They don't make the other side feel understood. What they heard the other side say is not what they meant.

Make sure the other side knows that you have listened before you respond. If they think you aren't listening or already have an answer, they will dismiss your response to their concern.

Many years ago, I was negotiating a speaking fee. The meeting planner said, "We would never pay that much money. That is much more than we have in our budget. In fact, last year we had a speaker that only cost $500. The president of our company got him."

I immediately wanted to justify my speaking fee. I wanted to tell the planner that Zig Ziglar's fee was $25,000, Les Brown's was at $30,000, and Tony Robbins was charging $50,000 for a speech. How could she possibly think that my speaking fee was unreasonable? But I kept my mouth shut.

The planner turned in a 180-degree direction. She said, "Of course the speaker last year was terrible. He didn't discuss the points he told us he would. He was boring, and part of the audience left in the middle of the speech. I guess when you pay peanuts, you get monkeys. OK, are you available on June 17?"

If I had pushed back against what I thought were unreasonable comments, I would have killed the negotiation. Because I listened and showed empathy, she talked herself out of her thinking and back into a negotiated outcome that worked for both of us.

3. Cushion the objection.

Let the other side know that you understand and empathize with what they are talking about. Overdo your empathy. When you respond with understanding and the other negotiator hears it, they may feel the concern is less important.

> **NEGOTIATOR 1:** That leaves us very little profit. I'm not sure I can go that far.
>
> **NEGOTIATOR 2:** I understand. That would concern me also. You worked very hard. You don't want to give all your profit away. I totally get it.

4. Question the objection.

I mentioned earlier that what you hear may not be what they meant. It's important to get the other side to clarify their meaning and intent. You may be answering the wrong question. You may need negotiating a point they don't care about.

Always ask, "What about X is a concern to you?" For example, "I know that money is an issue for you. What is your worry regarding that?"

Many years ago, I received a speaking fee objection. (The truth is, speaking fees are almost always negotiated.) I got a fairly straightforward objection: "Your speaking fee is too high. We can afford it."

I then said something crazy: "What about my speaking fee is too high?"

Surprisingly, the meeting planner said, "It's not your speaking fee; it's the airfare. The speaker last year charged your same speaking fee but also charged for first-class round-trip airfare from LA to New York City. The airfare alone was $3,500. We just can't afford that kind of expense."

By questioning the objection, I found out it wasn't about the fee; it was about the airfare. I guaranteed a much lower travel cost and booked the event.

Even though you hear an objection that seems straightforward, question it. It may not be what they meant to say.

NEGOTIATOR 1: What about tying your money up is a concern for you?

NEGOTIATOR 2: It's not really about tying my money up. In 2009, I was in the intensive care unit at a hospital for three weeks, and in the general care ward for a month after that. Even though we had health insurance, I still had to come up with nearly $15,000 in deductible and copays. I just don't want to be put in the position again where I have to scramble for the money to pay for emergencies.

5. Isolate the objection.

When you answer one objection, another is often waiting. Make sure you ask, "Is that your biggest worry, or is there something else that is more important?" This will ensure that you only answer one.

One of my clients was late to a coaching appointment. He had been wrestling over objections with his own client. After a few hours, the client finally said yes. I asked my client if he had bludgeoned his client into submission. "You can force a decision," I said, "but it will probably end up killing the deal the next day." That's exactly what happened. The client gave up and said yes just to get away.

To continue the example above:

NEGOTIATOR 1: Is liquidity and not wanting to scramble for
the money to pay for emergencies your biggest concern?
Or is there something else more important than that?

NEGOTIATOR 2: No, that's it. I just want to have enough
money to pay for emergencies.

6. Confirm the decision criteria.

Go back to the let's assume response. This is most important step
in answering negotiation objections. It is based on the information
you discovered in the probing phase. When we discussed the let's
assume technique, we asked, "Let's assume it's three years in the
future. What happened that let you know everything worked well,
and we had a great relationship?"

They gave you three responses. You drilled down from those
emotions to quantities. You then recapped and trial-closed to gain
commitment to accomplishing those goals. Now is when you bring
all that back to the negotiation.

If from the let's assume technique you discovered that a client
wanted to retire at sixty, here is how you would refer to that need.
"I know you think the fees are too high. Didn't you tell me that
retiring at sixty is critical? Is that still important to you?" This also
focuses the client back on the big picture.

NEGOTIATOR 1: Last week, during our meeting, you said
you had three very important goals. First, you wanted to
avoid running out of money during retirement. Second,

you wanted to decrease volatility. In fact, you didn't want to lose another penny from your portfolio. Third, you wanted to leave a legacy for your kids. Are these things still important to you?

NEGOTIATOR 2: Yes, very important.

7. Answer with logic; illustrate with a story.

Tell the other side about someone else who had the same concern and how you helped. The more you can get the other side to identify with the person in the story, the more effective it will be.

In any negotiation, a story does three things. First, it makes concepts more understandable. Second, it makes your points more memorable. Lastly, people connect emotionally to points in the story where they might not relate to a concept alone.

There's another reason stories are so effective: after the age of fifty-five, people tend to assimilate technical details much less effectively than when they were younger. In graduate school, I wouldn't take any notes in class. I would return home and write out the notes from three hours of lecture. I always got straight A's. Today, in my late sixties, I go to the restroom and can't remember why I walked in there. I'm exaggerating, but you get the point: We remember stories forever. Memory of concepts is fleeting.

To continue our example:

NEGOTIATOR 1: Well, I know it's important to you to have enough money for emergencies. Anybody who has gone through what you did would agree. It might be a great idea to set aside a portion of your portfolio, say $15,000, and keep it liquid. That way you'd fulfill your other needs. That will make your money last as long as you do, decrease volatility, and leave a legacy for your kids—all while still planning for emergencies.

During the Great Recession of 2008, one of my clients lost nearly 45 percent of her portfolio. Like you, she had a life-changing illness. Her heart attack almost killed her. Along with all that, she had a small stroke. Even today, you can see her how mouth turns down as she speaks. Yet she still had to plan for twenty years of retirement without being a burden to her children. She was old enough for Medicare and had a supplemental addition. We segmented $10,000 of her portfolio as liquid funds for emergencies. She could access it anytime she wanted. We put another 90 percent portfolio into the same kind of safe investment that we're talking about right now.

That was in 2008. Even though she has the emergency fund, she never had a reason to use it. Her safe portfolio is growing. The growth portion is building even faster. But now she has the comfort of knowing that she has a cushion in case an emergency happens. That's what I want for you.

8. Trial close.

This is a check on whether you've solved the problem. The trial close is critical to gaining the other side's commitment to resolving any issues. It also allows you to get the temperature of the water before you jump in.

You can ask, "Do you feel better about this now?" or "Did I answer that for you?" or "Did I solve that concern for you?" You could even say, "Does this work better for you?"

Never ask if they have any other questions. You've already answered an objection. You don't want to produce any others.

NEGOTIATOR 1: Did I answer that for you?
NEGOTIATOR 2: Yes, I think that might work.

9. Close.

The best time to conclude the negotiation is after you have successfully answered an objection. Not after a trial close, but after you have solved their concern. Closing should really be assumptive—mainly just writing up the paperwork. If they don't stop you, they've agreed to the deal.

Once you trial-close and they accept your offer, write up the deal immediately. If there's a contract to create, make sure that you're the one writing it. If it is simply paying and getting a receipt, initiate that immediately. Don't leave it to another day and risk procrastination. Don't let the other party sleep on it You've already covered that ground. You've already avoided the stall; don't give it another chance. Get the other side to conclude the agreement.

4

The Psychological Edge to Negotiation Success

I once heard the functional definition of *trust* as *the confidence another has that you will do what is best for them*. Without trust, the opposite happens. Without trust, you will reject a $100 bill offered by a stranger on the streets of New York City, thinking it's a trap. Trust is everything. With trust, you can get people to listen. Without trust, nothing is accomplished.

Since trust is such an important part of any negotiation, this chapter is dedicated towards how to establish and maintain trust in any negotiation. Not only will you find out how to gain trust, but also to check how much you have at any point during the negotiation. You will learn how to read the other side even before they tell you verbally what they think. You will be able to spot when the other side is lying, so you can ask relevant questions. You will learn how to push to get a desired outcome as well as on how to back off. You will even learn the most persuasive words in the English language and how to use them appropriately to achieve a negotiated outcome that is right for each side.

Psychological Edge 1: Trust Is the Key

Competence is still important. You need to have credibility. But people rarely buy based on those things alone. You also need to communicate that you also have the competence to do what is best for the other party. They must know that you can deliver on promises.

My wife has the competence to buy Christmas presents that everybody will enjoy, but I don't trust her to stay within our budget. This happens every year, and there's always a reason for it: the grandkids. Every grandparent loves to spoil grandchildren. It's what we do. But when a partner goes over budget on more important expenditures than Christmas presents, trust is broken.

How can you gain trust quickly during negotiations? People buy trust first, products and services second. I spoke at a seminar many years ago and asked the audience why and how people really decide to do business. I just got blank stares. I would give them a few choices. Was it price? Could they just undercut what the competition charges and always get business? Possibly, but someone is always willing to beat your price even if they have to take a loss.

Do customers buy because of speed of delivery, like with Amazon Prime? Do they buy because they can get double the quality at half the price? Sometimes during a speech, I single out a marketing VP and ask if they will allow their salespeople to cut prices by 25 percent and make up the difference with a higher volume of sales. Nearly every VP politely smiles and nods a firm no. I've actually managed to irritate a few CEOs who thought I was serious.

At that point, I usually follow up with a very simple question: "Please raise your hand if you think trust is the most important thing that you do." Nearly everybody responds yes. Then I ask if they know specifically, pragmatically, step-by-step, how to get trust. No hands go up. Jokingly I say, "Let me get this straight. You said that the most important thing you do is trust, but you're not even sure how to do it. Did I get that right?"

Isn't that the question? Isn't trust the most important thing we do in a negotiation? But isn't it also true that none of us are completely sure how to get it? Very few know how to get trust, aside from voicing platitudes like "Be honest" and "Show empathy."

HOW TO GAIN TRUST

People do business with those who are like them. We avoid those who are dissimilar. We tend not to trust those whose behavior we can't predict. People buy from people who act like them, talk like them, and even look like them. We avoid those with whom we don't share commonalities.

Suppose I am talking to somebody with whom I have a lot in common. Like me, they have grandkids like me, possibly play tennis and golf, and have advanced university degrees. Those characteristics are a very good start. That might be the beginning of a trust-based business relationship, but it takes more. More importantly, gaining trust has to do with whether you also share the traits of voice pace, pitch, rhythm, and tone. People trust people who are like them.

MATCHING AND MIRRORING

Let me give you an example: if I'm a fast-talking New Yorker on a conference call with a slower speaker from Alabama, there will be very little rapport in the beginning. If I talk a mile a minute to a colleague in Texas, there could also be a mismatch.

I need to match and mirror what I hear. If the other side of the negotiation speaks rapidly, I need to speed up. If they speak slowly, I need to modulate. People mirror people they trust. They avoid people they distrust.

In 1985, very early in my career, I was one of the first researchers to apply neurolinguistic programming (NLP) techniques in business. NLP is based on a model of how people communicate created by two researchers at the University of California, Santa Cruz: psychologist Richard Bandler and linguist John Grinder. One of the easiest applications of this new approach was gaining rapport. I couldn't wait to try it out.

When I was twenty-seven, I was on the phone at least five hours a day, calling all over the US. I am a naturally fast speaker, but I had no idea how much I mismatched listeners. Using NLP, I slowed down when I heard the other person pause. I sped up when I sensed they had a quick delivery. My business immediately increased. I could feel the connection. Every conversation seemed to flow better. If this seems far-fetched, you haven't been paying attention. When you generate more rapport, you also engender more trust. When you elicit trust, your negotiations become more successful.

Sometimes I'm asked whether matching and mirroring will cause people to feel mocked and manipulated. Yes, that could happen, if it is done poorly. For example, if you are a lightning-fast speaker and slow down abruptly, the change of pace will be noticed. A rule of thumb is to wait five to seven seconds. If you notice the other side is a fast speaker, speed up your voice pace over the next five to seven seconds. Or you could slow down during the same interval. If you wait more than seven seconds to match and mirror, nobody will ever think you are being disingenuous or manipulative.

Don't get caught up in thinking that successful negotiations are all about technical mechanics. You are still in the people business. It's all about rapport and trust. Everything else is tangential and secondary. Although gambits like waiting for the other side to make the first offer or playing the reluctant seller are useful, they are less important than your ability to engage. A successful negotiated outcome is all about rapport and trust. These are the most important aspects of negotiating any deal.

Putting people skills first is especially challenging to those who focus on product or technical knowledge. People revert to what they know. If they aren't educated and confident in their communication skills, they try to overwhelm people with product knowledge. It usually doesn't end well. You will never be able to reach the outcomes you want unless your people skills are good.

MATCHING AND MIRRORING NONVERBAL CUES

Just as you've learned how to match and mirror someone's voice, you can do the same with body movements. When the other party sits back in their chair, you should also. If they sit to the side, you should sit to the side too. If they prop their head in their hand, you should do the same.

Matching and mirroring to gain rapport and generate trust.

Does this work? Absolutely. Again, people gain rapport faster with those who are similar. They avoid those who are unlike them. Generating similarity applies not only to your background, values, morals, and education, but also to how you communicate. The more you talk like the other side, the more rapport you will gain. If you maintain rapport long enough, you will generate trust. Everything else being equal, trust is why people do deals with you.

In 1983, during the writing of my book *Sales Magic*, I attended a cocktail party the evening before a speech in Pasadena, California. I had been nominated by the US Junior Chamber of Commerce (Jaycees), a young adult (ages twenty to thirty-five) affiliate of the US Chamber of Commerce, as one of the most outstanding young men in America. I was a newly minted PhD and was only a couple of years removed from pro tennis tours. I also was just beginning my speaking career and must have looked like an easy mark.

The Jaycees were a nationwide organization that was always looking for speakers. The problem was, they had no budget. Although they were unable to pay speaking fees, they certainly had lots of free beer. No matter where you looked, a keg was close by. The audience numbered in the thousands. Of course, there were kegs of beer everywhere in the conference room. This was the one and only time I have seen conference attendees clumped around kegs of beer. It has never happened since.

During the cocktail party the evening before my speech, I spoke about the event to the president of the group. I had a beer in my right hand and was propped against the doorjamb with my right shoulder. After my second glass, I noticed the president holding his beer in the same hand, and leaning against a door as well. Since I was so aware of matching and mirroring, our mutual mirroring hit me like a ton of bricks.

I started to notice the flow of the conversation. We were both having a lot of fun and had great rapport. We could have talked for a couple of hours. The rapport was so thick that one attendee walked in front of us swaying in the hallway, obviously drunk. The president and I raised our eyebrows and glasses at the same time, glad that that wasn't us.

At that moment, I tried something crazy. I purposely mismatched. I moved my left shoulder against the opposite doorjamb. I even switched the hand holding the beer. I waited to see what the president would do. It took a while, but he unconsciously mirrored me back. What seemed like an eternity took only twenty seconds.

MIRRORING: BUILDING TRUST NONVERBALLY

A landmark project conducted at the University of Utah in the late seventies included videotape studies of parents bringing their children to school. One sequence involved a father and child. The father brought his daughter to the door and opened it for her. Before going inside, the little girl turned around to wave good-bye. He waved back, and she turned around again and went inside. The father closed the door and left. The entire sequence took about three seconds, and there seemed to be nothing extraordinary about it.

When viewed in slow motion, however, the film revealed some very interesting interactions. When the daughter turned to wave good-bye to her father, she began to approach him. At the very same moment, the father raised his hand. The author of the study wrote that this movement was not only the beginning of the father's own wave, but that it resembled the motion of a policeman stopping traffic at an intersection. The effect on the little girl seemed to be the same. She stopped moving forward just as the palm of her father's hand was facing her. At the end of his wave, when the father began putting his hand down, she turned around to head back inside the school.

To the research, viewing the film in slow motion made it seem as though the father was pushing his daughter away. "Even though there was no actual physical connection between father and daughter," he wrote, "they looked like puppets that are being manipulated by the same strings." Reviewing the sequence further, he realized that the father was in a hurry, so it was more important for him to get his daughter inside the school and be on his way.

This little sequence shows how we communicate without words. At an unconscious level, we mirror and match each other's movements as we send and receive information. When you can learn to read others' nonverbal signals and communicate back to them in the same way, you take rapport to a very deep level. As you will see later on in this book, you can use such physical techniques to pace your meeting and lead your customer to a successful conclusion.

Studies of nonverbal signals have shown how powerful unconscious communication is. If I had to choose one thing that helps negotiators do so well, this would be it. Without even realizing it, they mirror clients and match movements at every opportunity. It's what gives them such high rapport. This lays the groundwork for the seemingly effortless negotiation later on.

Mirroring, or matching body movements is, for example, crossing one's legs when the other person does. If one puts her hands on the table, the other does the same. In videotape studies we have conducted, we have noticed that when people are getting along, they not only match body movement but voice tone and speed as well. It's as if they are trying to be more like each other, hoping to cut out all differences. To really see mirroring in action, watch two people who are in love. They gaze into each other's eyes, stay as close together as possible, and mirror each other's movements, no matter how small or insignificant. They create what has been called the *romantic dance*.

Adversaries, on the other hand, will unconsciously mismatch. If one person is leaning forward, the other will lean back. If one has her hands on her hips, the other will put hers at her side. Adversaries will also break eye contact rather than allow rapport to build.

Mirroring also occurs in groups. When someone is liked or highly regarded, others tend to do the same. If you watch closely, you can learn to spot the leaders in any group. Of course, crossing one's arms may simply indicate that they're cold, though I've seen the same happen when temperature wasn't a factor.

Learn to pay attention to the different movements people make when they are talking with you. After waiting for a few seconds, mirror them. You can learn how to do this without skipping a beat in your conversation.

Mirroring sounds so simple that people often have a hard time believing it works. Try the following experiment. The next time you are at a restaurant, mirror your dining partner. If he has his head in his hands, put your head in your hands. If she crosses her legs with the right over the left, do the same. If his head is cocked to one side, mirror that. After a few minutes, that person will be following you.

I recently heard a story about a consulting psychologist who was enormously skilled in these techniques. She was called upon by a Realtor who wanted help negotiating a fee the Realtor felt was due from a past employer. Apparently, the Realtor had sold a few properties with the understanding that she would get a $10,000 commission. Her old boss had never paid it, claiming that they had negotiated a different arrangement.

The Realtor asked the psychologist if she could attend the meeting with the old boss. At first, the boss balked at having a third party present, but finally agreed as long as she didn't say a word to the Realtor.

During the entire meeting, the consultant mirrored the Realtor's boss. Whenever he said something positive or conciliatory, the consultant would match his posture. Whenever he said something negative or counterproductive, the consultant mismatched his posture. After about forty minutes, the Realtor's old employer conceded and agreed to pay the Realtor the $10,000 owed.

The funny thing was that at the end of the meeting, the employer apologized to the consultant, saying, "It's too bad you had to sit silently through all this." Obviously, the boss had no idea of the enormous influence the consultant had over him by simply matching and mismatching his movements.

I experience this kind of situation often. I once spoke at a sales conference in northern California. The morning before my presentation, I had breakfast with another speaker on the program. Thinking about my speech and yet not wanting to appear rude, I spoke little, listened reflectively, and tried to maintain rapport by mirroring instead. I crossed my arms when he crossed his. I crossed my legs when he did. I leaned forward when he did. At the end of breakfast, he said he loved my ideas and asked me to speak to his company about communication skills.

I had said virtually nothing. Again, I saw how people are persuaded by what they hear themselves say, not from what the other person says. Rapport—and the nonverbal communication that develops from it—is the all-important factor. Because the rapport between us was so high, I had created an opportunity without even intending to.

Mirroring generates a tremendous amount of rapport. Along with rapport comes trust. And when you gain trust, you get business.

CALIBRATING

Because it is a result of high rapport, mirroring is also an excellent way for you to check whether you are connecting with your negotiation partner. You can tell if both of you are in the same ballpark by the way they match your movements. If you say or do something the other side doesn't like, mismatching will start to occur and mirroring will stop. This is extremely useful in determining what people like and don't like about your ideas.

Noticing what someone does when they are interested in what you have to say is called *calibration*. We all notice things like a smile when someone is happy and a frown when someone is sad. Start paying attention to other nonverbal cues as well. It usually takes about two minutes before I start picking out different behavioral nuances in a conversation. If someone leans back in her chair while I am talking, she could be showing negativity or defensiveness. Or perhaps she needs some time to absorb my ideas. In either case, it tells me to back off for a bit.

Using both verbal and nonverbal techniques together is the heart of unconscious competence. You verify what you learn from one technique and build upon it with another. Eventually, you sense exactly what is being communicated to you.

Paying attention to nonverbal cues is one of the toughest lessons for negotiators to learn. They often aren't aware of someone's level of interest because they aren't thinking of anything but what they want to say. Remember that negotiation is a relationship: for the process to be effective, you want to be aware of what the other side is communicating throughout. When you let it become second nature, you will be much more aware of what to say and when to say it. You'll know whether you are on the right track or whether it is time to change something in your presentation.

CROSSOVER MIRRORING

I get letters from readers who are nervous about mirroring. They think it implies mockery. Or they're afraid negotiation partners will think of mirroring as copying. Or they think that instead of producing higher rapport, mirroring will make the other side negative or hostile.

To counter the argument, I always remind them of the underlying premise: if you really have the other side's best interests at heart and are operating on a win/win paradigm, they will sense it in everything you do. Instead of copying your clients, you will be drawing them out. The other party will always be focused on the words rather than on the nonverbal signals of your conversation. They will not notice what you are doing.

If you are reluctant to try mirroring right off, I suggest something softer and less obtrusive: *crossover mirroring*.

Crossover mirroring is mirroring a gesture with a different part of the body. In other words, if someone crosses their arms, then you cross your legs. If their head is resting on a hand, then you might touch your chin. If someone has his hands in his pockets, then you fold your hands in your lap very close to your pockets. If they tap a pencil, you can twirl a pen in your hands.

Crossover mirroring is particularly useful when men and women are negotiating. If you want to match someone's movements but feel it would be inappropriate, try crossover mirroring. For example, people wearing pants feel comfortable crossing their legs in a more open fashion; a woman wearing a dress would mirror this by crossing her legs more tightly. Men feel comfortable leaning back and clasping their hands behind their head. A woman can lean back without clasping her hands behind her head. She can keep them at her sides to show an open attitude.

MATCHING VOICE PATTERNS

A number of years ago at a book convention, I was discussing some ideas with another writer. He was very successful, and I was hoping to pick up a few tips and business leads from him. Unfortunately, our rapport was low. He seemed distracted and tired (as everybody seems to become at conventions). He also had a high-pitched voice, almost a squeak, which made it hard to hear him on top of everything else.

I have a lower, fairly resonant voice. After talking to him for a few minutes and getting nowhere, I raised my voice a little, trying to sound more like him. It was interesting to see how quickly he warmed up to me. We ended up having a conversation that I suspect was much more productive than it otherwise would have been.

Your voice is one of your best tools for establishing rapport. You can match someone's pace, pitch, timbre, or inflections.

Pace is the speed of your voice. Some people talk more quickly than others. On average, we speak at about 125 words per minute, although this average varies depending on the part of the country in which we live.

Pitch is how high or low your voice is. You can sound like a parakeet, or as low as a tuba player playing a John Philip Sousa march.

Timbre is the resonance of your voice. Actor James Earl Jones, for example, has a very resonant voice. It is full and rich, projecting into every corner of the theater, and is part of what makes him such a great actor.

Word inflections also vary from person to person, as syllables are emphasized, shortened, or drawn out. Think of all the different accents we have in the US, from the clipped, staccato style of the New Englander to the Texas twang to the drawl of the Deep South.

Listen intently to your negotiation partner for the first three or four minutes of your conversation. Make a note of everything you hear: word inflections, the length of their sentences, how loud or soft their voices are. Even attend to how they mark out key words. Pick out what you find distinctive, and try to match it. It will make your clients feel much more at ease with you.

This is particularly important if you negotiate in different parts of the country. Be aware of accents and other little regional idiosyncrasies. People expect you to talk like them. When you don't, your listeners will be distracted by trying to adjust to the sound of your voice. This can create tension, waste time, and cause misunderstandings.

About one year into my speaking career, I spoke in a rural area, where everyone spoke fairly slowly. My speech cadence is in a fast-paced urban style. I was thirty minutes into my hour-long program when a man in the back row raised his hand. I didn't want to stop my speech for questions, because I had a limited amount of time, so I ignored him. Unfortunately, he kept his hand raised for about seven to ten minutes straight and started distracting the people around him. I finally called on the man and asked if he had a question. He sat back in his chair, put his thumbs in his belt, and said in a very loud drawl, "Son, I'd like to know what you said after you said hello."

Obviously I was speaking too fast and had developed little rapport. If I thought I was getting any message across to this man, and probably to many others in the room, I was sadly mistaken. I was wasting my time and theirs.

When you talk to someone on the phone, pay particular attention. The speed of their voice is usually the first thing you notice. Adjust your pace to match theirs. Also listen to their speech patterns. You won't be able to duplicate someone's voice exactly. But the more you match, the less jarring you will sound to the person at the other end.

In the late seventies, I had an unsuccessful stock brokering career. In our office was a broker named Sam, who did more business than the rest of the office combined. Sam had enormous girth. He smoked cigars. He had a wonderful personality—if he liked you, he'd blow smoke in your face as he talked to you. If he didn't like you, he'd spit the cigar butt at you. But Sam was great on the phone. If his client had a high-pitched voice, he'd increase the pitch of his voice. If a client spoke slowly, Sam would slow down. If a customer was loud, we'd hear Sam's voice booming into the phone. He even knew how to giggle like a teenager. I don't think Sam did it consciously. He knew how to mimic his clients without offending them. And he made millions.

THE TRUST CHECK

Once you have rapport in a negotiation, there is a natural inclination to maintain it. If you mismatch while in rapport, the other person will try to mirror you back in an attempt to continue trust.

Generally, you can check how much trust you have by purposely mismatching, then notice whether they follow. If they mirror you back, you have an enormous amount of rapport. If they don't, go back to mirroring. Wait a while, and try to mismatch again.

Thirty years ago, I received a letter from my client John Milam in Knoxville, Tennessee. John had heard me speak a couple of times and said he was a fan. One day he showed up at a potential partner's office about ten minutes early. The man was thirty minutes late, making John wait for nearly forty minutes. As he approached John, both arms were crossed. John immediately crossed his arms in response. The potential partner said, "I'm sorry I'm late. But I don't have time to meet with you today." Both had their arms crossed, mirroring each other.

John said, "No problem. Would you like to reschedule?"

Something clicked in the partner's head. He said, "How long will it take if I see you right now?"

John said, "Ten minutes, unless you ask me any questions."

They walked back to the office. The potential partner settled into a big wing-backed chair. John sat in a smaller one in front of the desk. The guy said, "You have ten minutes, go!"

After five minutes, he reclined and crossed his fingers behind his head.

Guess what John did? John mirrored back. He leaned back and crossed his fingers behind his head. John wrote they both looked like a couple of plucked chickens.

But then John did something crazy: he leaned forward on the desk. John actually invaded his negotiation partner's personal space. Crazy, unless the person does guess what? He followed John, leaning forward on his own desk. This is called a trust check. If you mismatch and notice that the other person mirrors you back, you have used the trust check to see how much trust you have. If you see this, stop talking. If you keep talking, you will oversell and buy it back.

When you begin a negotiation, first match and mirror. If they speak quickly, speed up your pace. If the other side talks slowly, throttle down after a seven-second interval.

Once you have matched and mirrored the other side, check how much trust you have from time to time by, for example, speaking with a burst of speed and seeing if they follow. You could also slow down to check whether they mirror you back. Using this technique may seem complex in the beginning, but isn't it worth it to check how much trust you have? Employing this skill set will make you a much better listener.

Listening is the first step to making any one involved in a negotiation feel understood. Most research has shown this is the beginning of rapport. At that point trust comes a lot more naturally. After trust, everything else is easy.

Psychological Edge 2: How to Spot a Lie

How good are your probing skills? Can you read someone's thoughts, or are you just listening to their words? Probing is the most important part of the process of reaching successful negotiated outcomes. The better you probe, the less you have to close. The better you probe, the less you need to persuade. But if you are like most people, you blindly accept the other side's comments and responses to your questions.

John, a successful financial advisor, greeted some new prospective clients at an initial appointment, which was really an introductory get-together to determine whether there was enough trust to move forward. He hoped to interest the clients enough to pay a planning fee and move to the next phase of implementing a financial plan.

After some initial pleasantries, John asked the couple what their retirement goals were. They said they were worried about running out of money and the volatility of the past year.

John knew enough to qualify the couple and asked if there were working with another advisor. They said yes. He asked when they had last spoken to the advisor. The husband looked up at the ceiling and said, "Not for a long time."

John finished the rest of the meeting and asked if the couple wanted to proceed. The husband responded, "Let us go think about it and we will get back to you."

After a few weeks of follow-up calls, John finally connected and asked if they wanted to book another appointment. The husband said he had an advisor they liked a lot and only wanted a few new ideas to share with him.

John wondered what he could have missed. Could he have qualified better? Was there a question he should have asked? The couple wasn't completely honest in the meeting. How could he have missed this? Is there something else he could have said?

The answer lies in your emotional intelligence (EQ). Are you listening for content and context? More importantly, can you read behavior well enough to find out whether people are being completely honest?

Twenty years ago, I spoke at a conference on "How to Read Your Client's Mind." An FBI agent spoke after me on how important it was to spot lies during witness field interviews. One fabrication could send the whole investigation down a rabbit hole. FBI agents employ an involved method of reading body language and spotting stress, which suggests a need for more questions.

You don't need the advanced training of an FBI field agent to spot the truth. There is a better way. My 1980s book *Sales Magic* was the first to describe a business application of the three types of perceptual communication styles as taught by NLP: visual, auditory, and kinesthetic. Visual individuals make sense of what you say by producing images from your words. Auditories gain understanding and rapport by listening to how you sound. Kinesthetics gain trust by how they feel with you.

You can diagnose each mode by noticing someone's eyes and words. Visuals move their eyes up to the right when thinking about the future. They move their eyes up to the left when recalling the past. Auditory people move their eyes to the right when thinking about what to say. They move their eyes to the left side when recalling past conversations. Kinesthetics are simple to spot, because their eyes move down to the right when they get a feeling.

Since visuals and auditory people move their eyes to the right when constructing future thoughts, and to the left when recalling memories, you can spot fabrications in their responses if you closely pay attention.

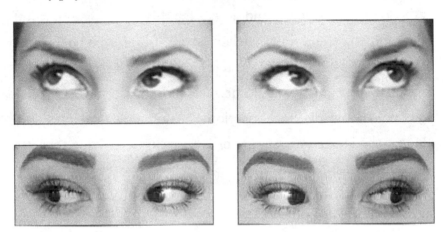

The direction of eye movements reveal an individual's personal communication style.

Let's say you ask a negotiation partner if they are working with anyone else on a deal. They will look left as they recall the person. Let's also say you ask about the last time they spoke to that person. In response, they look right, making up an answer. *When you ask about something from the past and someone thinks in the future, their response is a fabrication. It is a lie.*

Not every fabrication is a purposeful deception. If you ask where I live, I will likely look up to the right and say Charleston, South Carolina, especially if you aren't familiar with the Southeast.

The truth is, I don't live in Charleston. But trying to be helpful, I think about a large nearby location to make the conversation easier. If you were aware of my eyes moving up to the right, you might say, "Do you live in Charleston or just close by?" I would then say, "Well, actually, I live in Daniel Island, next door to Charleston."

Think of the power you would have if you could spot fabrications when engaged in a negotiation. The question could be, "What is the lowest price you would accept for this?" This is important because if you could find out their lowest price in the beginning, you would know how your counteroffer would be accepted. If they look up to the right and say, "The lowest I could accept is $25,000," you would know that is a fabrication. You might respond by saying, "Is that the lowest you can go, or is there another issue that is a problem?"

Spotting a lie isn't about inelegantly accusing someone of being untruthful. It is giving you a tool to probe more effectively and a heightened ability to read the other side's emotions. It enables you to gain more rapport and avoid wasting your time.

Psychological Edge 3: Buying Signals

Whether you are playing the reluctant buyer or seller, don't over-react. Be sincere. Don't show your enthusiasm. Negotiation is as much about reading emotions as about the gambit used. Think of negotiation as a poker game. One of ESPN Sports' most popular shows is *World Championship Poker*. Five players gathered around the table do as much as they possibly can to avoid showing emotion. At the same time, every player is trying to spot "tells."

What does a player look like with a good hand? What non-verbal cues do they show when they are upset?

Nearly every player wears dark sunglasses or a low visor to keep others from seeing their eyes. Pupil dilation is involuntary. They dilate during enthusiasm and constrict during stress, anxiety and disappointment. Trained poker players will always admit that the game is more about psychology than poker skill.

You undoubtedly wouldn't know to avoid negotiating with someone wearing sunglasses or a low visor. You might not even look for pupil dilation as a buying signal. But if you don't spot these cues, you may not get the best deal.

Recently, a very bright and articulate salesperson presented the perfect product to a qualified and interested prospect. Kevin, the prospect, had been referred to John, the salesman, by a mutual friend. In fact, the referral was so strong that John skated through the approach and rapport phase of the sales cycle. During the probing phase of their conversation, he discovered that Kevin had a great need for his product. John presented it masterfully. He tailored each feature exactly to Kevin's needs. John was proud of the technical expertise he displayed during the presentation.

Unfortunately, John kept talking and talking . . . and talking, until Kevin looked anxiously at his watch. He cut short the interview on the premise that he had another appointment scheduled.

What went wrong? There is more to a deal than just probing and presenting. You have to be able to read emotions during a negotiation. You have to be able to read what someone is thinking before they say it.

As I've noted, many experts believe that communication is 83 percent nonverbal. That means only 17 percent is communicated verbally. There are so many misunderstandings partly because we tend to rely more on the words than on the totality of what is being communicated. This means matching words with body language for what is called *congruency*. Are the words in line with the speaker's body language? For example, is someone giving you a compliment while frowning? Does someone tell you how much they enjoy your company while looking away? These are examples of a lack of congruency.

Most books on negotiation discuss tactics, gambits, and strategies. Rarely do they discuss the psychological aspects of how to communicate more effectively. Body language enables you to understand the meaning and intent of what the other side is communicating. If you can ask the right questions and read body language, your negotiation will be much more successful and progress more quickly.

HOW TO RECOGNIZE WHEN THE DEAL IS DONE

Have you ever oversold? Have you ever talked your prospect right into—and out of—a deal? Here is a sentence that will double or triple your business this year if you apply it:

Negotiate in a way the other side wants to hear, not the way you want to present. Communicate in a way that will get the best results with the person you're speaking to.

Have you ever been in a business deal with someone who at one point seemed interested but suddenly had a meeting to go to?

Have you ever left a negotiation completely sure that it was a done deal, only to be nibbled or even canceled the next day? These are all examples of *noncongruency.*

As obvious as this may seem, research has shown that up to 30 percent of all negotiations are lost because the presenter didn't know when to stop talking. Knowing *when* is as, or more, important as *how.* Psychologists believe that every single behavior the other side displays gives you information you can use to negotiate a deal. The following cues will arm you with the ability to recognize when the other side wants to say yes.

Head Nod and Smile

The most basic of buying signals are a smile and a "yes" head-nodding motion.

Although this does not necessarily mean the person will say yes at that precise moment, this behavior pattern indicates that they have accepted your idea. But the faster you see their head nod, the more they are thinking, "I wish this guy would shut up!" Through the nod, they are saying, "I've heard this all before. Move on before I start to get bored."

At this moment, you should ask, "I sense this is pretty familiar to you. Where have you heard it before?" Proud to display their knowledge, the other side of the negotiation will clue you in about what they already know.

Pupil Dilation

While the head nod is obvious, this next buying signal is not. Extensive videotaped interviews indicate that when nude photos are shown, the viewer's pupils will expand with excitement and enthusiasm.

You might be thinking, "Kerry, I don't get close enough to see pupils." You ought to. No matter what the light level, most of your negotiation partners will involuntarily display pupil dilation when they are enthusiastic about your ideas.

Do you remember the expression on your children's faces at Christmas? They came out of their rooms and said, "Mommy, Daddy, is that for me?" Their eyebrows rose in gleeful joy. Did you ever see their eyes become round as saucers as their pupils dilated with pleasure?

Aristotle Onassis, the late Greek shipping tycoon, was rumored to always wear sunglasses during heavy business negotiations. If he didn't have his sunglasses, he would postpone his business meeting until he found a pair. He would also refuse to negotiate if his adversary was wearing sunglasses.

Is pupil dilation important? You bet. Unfortunately, Americans are usually not taught to notice such nuances. One reason the Russians and Chinese often best us in arms negotiations is that they are taught to pay attention to such behavioral nuances, which they believe are windows to inner emotions.

PROXEMICS

This is the study of personal space. The closer people are, the more comfortable they feel with each other. The greater the distance, the less comfortable and more defensive they feel. If you see a great friend, you may hug in a greeting. Someone you met recently might get a handshake. But if a great deal of rapport was generated, an arm on the back along with a handshake would be well received. It all depends on the level of rapport.

These details depend on cultural contexts. In Finland, for example, even a handshake may be too forward in a first meeting.

Distances of three feet and greater show a level of low comfort and rapport. This is a *stranger area*. It often occurs at first meetings or with someone you don't feel comfortable around.

A distance of two to three feet between you and a negotiation partner is an *acquaintance space*. It isn't a stranger area, nor is it an area reserved for trust. But it could progress to more rapport and trust later. A distance of one to two feet is a *buying space*. This occurs when someone is very interested in what you have to say and desires to hear more. It can also be a buying signal. If you see a negotiation partner move into one to two feet of you, they are unconsciously in acceptance of your idea. Zero to one feet is reserved for intimacy. When you get too

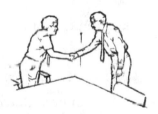

close, others will turn their shoulder to you in order to create more space between you.

Displays of Possessiveness

One of the most sophisticated buying signals is how someone shows
ownership with handouts and
illustrations. Do you give people
illustrations to look at? They may
glance over the sheet of paper and set it down. They may return it to your side of the conference table or even push it away. With any of these behaviors, the other side is showing psychological dispos-sessiveness. They are signaling, "The idea is not very impressive. My trust in you is low. I don't buy it." If you see this nonverbal cue, you may wish to go back to the probing stage. Find out their real need and/or desire. Don't even try to reach a deal yet.

On the other hand, the potential buyer may look at an illustra-tion for a few moments, then lay the sheet on their side of the table or desk, or even clutch it and say, "Is this my copy?" The message is obvious.

I once went on an appointment with an inexperienced nego-tiator. During the presentation stage, the other side was given a fact sheet. He immediately drew it closer. He was enormously pos-sessive of the sheet and kept it without asking for a copy. To my amazement, the inexperienced businessperson continued the pre-sentation for more than forty-five minutes.

I saw the other side go from moderate interest to apathy. In the course of one hour, I watched the new negotiator talk the other side in and back out of a deal. If you stop talking at the right time, your negotiations will become smoother and successful.

Chin Rubbing

During the process of evaluation, most people will show nonverbal signs indicating they are in deep thought. One will scratch their head, while another may tense his lips. The most overt of these decision signals is the chin rub.

When you see this behavior, *stop talking immediately.* The other side is deciding whether or not to accept your idea. If you keep talking, you'll only serve to confuse and intimidate. If you see this nuance, stop talking, wait for a few seconds, and trial-close by saying something like, "Does this approach seem right so far?" Of course, you might still hear an objection. But you'll be surprised how many will say yes at this point—all because you knew when to stop talking.

The Whistling Teapot and Sitting Tremor Positions

The most common buying signal you will see is leaning forward. Through numerous hours of video playback, we have noticed an intriguing relationship between the way people sit and their level of interest.

Most great negotiators understand when that the other side sits back, with his arms folded and legs crossed, they aren't very receptive. But when that same person moves forward or sits on the

edge of a chair—the whistling teapot position—they have emotionally already said yes.

An even more dramatic acceptance
position than the whistling teapot is the
sitting tremor signal.

It is also depicted by leaning forward
or sitting on the edge of a chair.

In this case, the other side has one
hand on a knee and the other forearm on a thigh. These people
may be so enthusiastic, they look as though they are about to
explode any moment.

The sitting tremor is a lot like the whistling teapot. It is also displayed by moving forward in their chair or leaning in toward you.
They are signaling, "Stop talking already; let me say yes."

This rule does not always apply. If your negotiation partner sits
forward in his chair the whole time, their back may just be sore.
But if you suddenly see them move forward, you've got a deal coming to a conclusion—as long as you stop talking and trial-close at
the right time.

Verbal Cues

Verbal buying signals are even more obvious. You have heard them
over the phone without even knowing it. Verbal buying signals are
statements such as "How much does this cost?" "Can I get this in
blue?" "How quickly can I get delivery?" "What kind of guarantee
does this come with?" All of these signal that the other side has
heard enough and wants you to stop talking.

Like with nonverbal cues, you should trial-close when you hear a verbal buying signal. I watched one negotiator spot a buying signal and then trial-close. The other side said, "Great, let's do it."

She then startled me by saying, "Are you sure?"

The other side then responded with, "I don't know. Shouldn't I be?"

And the salesperson was off to the races to recover.

Negotiation is all about probing for needs, providing solutions, and then getting people to accept your recommendations. Most of the time the other side will show and tell you when they are ready to say yes. If you miss those cues, you may miss doing a deal. Pay attention.

Craig Beachnaw, a top negotiator in Lansing, Michigan, almost missed one of the biggest deals of his career. The other side, a successful business owner, seemed to be giving buying signals. Craig determined needs the first day and presented his solutions on the second day. An hour in, the business owner moved into the sitting tremor position. Craig remembered my video on buying signals and decided to stop talking. Craig pulled the agreement out and used a simple trial close. The business owner signed it immediately.

Craig took him out to dinner that night and asked him why he said yes so quickly. The owner said that he had been ready thirty minutes before Craig stopped talking. He admitted that Craig was actually talking him out of the deal. Craig was buying it back!

If you watch for buying signals, you'll increase business by at least 30 percent. Million-dollar producers all admit that knowing *when* is as important as knowing *how*.

THE SKEPTIC

In a one-to-one negotiation, have you had the impression that the other side didn't quite agree with something you just said? Did they seem a bit skeptical? Or didn't seem to believe it? The problem is, by the time they tell you what they didn't agree with, it's too late.

Wouldn't you love to know what people are thinking at the time they're thinking it? Have you ever seen people move their glasses down the bridge of their nose? Or have you ever seen people look over the tops of their glasses? If they don't wear glasses, they'll look out from under their eyebrows.

These people are in disagreement. They don't believe you, or they don't understand what you are saying. They want you to prove it to them. When the other side displays one of these behaviors, say, "I can tell something about this is bothering you. Tell me what it is." They will immediately let you know. If you can stay credible throughout the negotiation, you will keep them in agreement. If you can keep them in accord most or all of the time, the negotiation will progress much more smoothly.

I did a speech years ago for Transamerica, an insurance company. An agent came up to me afterwards and said, "Kerry, I see this all the time. I know I'm in trouble when they take their glasses off and stare at me." He added, "I know I'm really in trouble when they take their contact lenses out."

This humor only displays the negotiation partner's need of making sure you stay on track. Always try to read the emotion from the other side.

Psychological Edge 4: Stress Cues

Here's a tough question. Do you think of yourself as a little bit pushy? Are you a hard closer? You're probably thinking that it's bad to push, but that may be short-sighted. It's good to be pushy at the right time. You just have to know when to push and when the other side is feeling pushed.

Someone once asked me, "Kerry, what about these hard closers, these door-to-door, Fuller Brush salesmen of yesteryear? They're just outmoded, aren't they?"

No, they're not. If you can push and back off at the right time, you're going to treat people the way they want to be treated and negotiate the way they want to be negotiated with. There's a time and place to push people, but you also need to know when to back off.

Sometimes people get relationship stress: they feel uneasy when talking about their money or other issues. Negotiation itself may cause some level of psychological stress.

People may do two things to let you know that they're feeling pushed, pressed, and stressed.

Here are three signals people use to let you know when you are closing too hard. These signals will show you when the other side is feeling pushed, stressed, or uneasy. If you learn how to determine when people are feeling these emotions, you can back off, gain more information, and push at a better time.

Here are three things people do when you have miscalculated and pushed too hard:

1. When people are feeling pushed, they will rub their forehead back and forth.

2. When prospects feel pressed, they will break eye contact for more than a couple of seconds.

3. When people feel stressed, they will blink their eyes rapidly, more than forty times per minute.

FBI research has shown that when people lie, they feel stress. When we feel stress, we most readily show it in our blink rate.

There are also three verbal signals that your negotiation partner is stressed.

1. **Vacuous conversation.** They will talk but say nothing. For example, "I guess that is a good idea, but I think, maybe we should sort of . . ."

   In other words, they talk but say nothing substantial, even though they may have started out as fluid conversationalists. This is the beauty of calibrating in the beginning of the relationship: if vacuous conversation is a change in behavior from someone who was initially articulate, it is a stress cue.

2. **Pregnant pauses.** When people feel stressed, they pause for long periods—often twenty seconds or more.

3. **Stuttering and stammering.** This is also a sign of stress if the person was articulate at the beginning.

A few years ago, I was in a church in El Paso, Texas, speaking on coping with stress. The minister was enormously popular. He jokingly said his church had six commandments and four do-the-best-you-cans.

After I was done, the minister got up and did a fifteen-minute push on his congregation. "I want all you sinners to dedicate your selves to the Lord tonight. Can I have an amen on this?"

As I looked down at the audience, I saw three people in the front row rubbing their foreheads. What are people thinking when they use this gesture? Do they just have an itch? They're showing unease and stress.

What do you do when you see gestures like this? A woman approached me at a presentation in Toronto and said, "Kerry, I was giving a presentation. The decision maker started rubbing his forehead. I thought the guy had an itch. But then I remembered what you said about reading stress cues. I stopped talking and said, 'I can tell you're feeling uneasy about this. Would you like to share your thoughts?'"

The point is not using these specific words; the point is knowing *when* to use them. If you can pull emotions out of your negotiation partners at the right time, they'll tell you things they won't tell their spouses; they'll put that much trust in you. When they do that, you have a lifelong client rather than a one-shot customer.

John was in the middle of talking to a couple about transferring their pension plan to his company to manage. The investment business hadn't been especially great lately, and John had already spent his commission. This time the previous year, John was closing about three clients a week for about $6,000 in commissions. All he had to do before was answer the phone. Now he would be lucky to close three a month.

Now he has to visit prospects and look them in the eye. My, how things have changed! John had to learn to read people better. But these prospects were perfect. They had had retirement goals, made a good living, and needed financial planning. All he had to do was negotiate his fees. He was ready to offer a free financial plan if they would only say yes. He could already count the fees he would make. John laid out the package and filled out the application form. He worked for the next week lining up all the details. When he called the couple back, they apologized but said they went with another financial advisor.

What happened? The deal was right, the prospects were qualified, John was able to gain rapport. What went wrong? John didn't read the signals. The couple were showing stress cues John didn't pay attention to.

Years ago, when I spoke at an insurance conference, the top salesperson said that 100 percent of his prospects say yes to him. I was amazed. I asked what closing techniques he used. He couldn't name one. Like most top producers, he was an unconscious competent. I pushed him harder. He admitted that he didn't really know that much about sales, but he did know how to read people better than most of his competitors. I asked what he looked for. He didn't know. I asked what he listened to. He still didn't know, but he knew it when he saw it.

Such is the case with top producers. They have been around so long they know how to put big numbers on the board, but it's all unconscious. They know how to do deals but couldn't tell you how, what, or when.

Whenever I speak at a conference, there is always one top producer who headlines the event and tells the audience exactly what they have heard 100 times before. That is because the peak performers can't communicate how they do it. It takes a psychologist to convey the information. And here it is.

Xerox research has shown that the average sales negotiation includes three rejections and objections. The surprising truth is that most producers will stop after the first rejection. They also stop pressing when they feel they are pushing, not when the other side feels pressed.

If you can see John Smith through John Smith's eyes, you can sell John Smith what John Smith buys. John Smith will buy a lot from someone who understands him and reads between the eyes.

Psychological Edge 5: The Twelve Most Persuasive Words to Use When Negotiating

Yale University researchers have found key words that will help people understand concepts better, retain information longer, and remember details better. These words are more persuasive than any other words in the English language. They can be used in website content, email blasts, electronic brochures, and pre-approach letters, and will increase response rates. Information associated with these words will be retained longer. In fact, Madison Avenue is using these words in social media advertising and other media. Using these twelve words will work for your message as well. They will not only grab attention but cause the other side to retain your message longer. You should use these words in emails and any other communication with the other side of the negotiation. They are:

1. **Discovery.** Many years ago, Sears created a new credit card. They did years of research on the words most capable of conveying the highest impact. Sears was on the verge of bankruptcy when they sold the card off and raised enough revenue to survive. The card is still successful today. It's the Discover card.

   Sears wasn't the only company to profit from this word. Ford's top SUVs twenty years ago were the Expedition and Explorer. Their only competition was a vehicle from Land Rover. What a coincidence. It is still called the Discovery.

   Here is how you could use this word in a negotiation: "I have *discovered* a concept that will meet all your goals." "If we could talk about this new *discovery*, would that help?"

2. **Easy.** You will buy a car every five years or lease one every 2.5 years. Auto manufacturers make about $500 in profit from the sale of a sedan and $2,500 from a lease. They get you to lease rather than buy by using the word *easy*. Such as, "Easy terms, easy qualifying, easy to drive." *Easy* is the word online car dealers like Carvana and Vroom use to get your attention. Their message is to buy online and make the process easy; you will have absolutely no trouble. The word *easy* is also used to sell mortgages, home rentals, and even complex software. In

a negotiation, you might say, "Here are some ideas that will make this process *easy* for you."

3. **Guarantee.** "I guarantee this or your money back!" "It'll work; I'll stake my reputation on it." "I guarantee it will be effective for you."

   You can't guarantee investment returns, but you can guarantee a relationship. When negotiating, you might say, "I *guarantee* you will be happy with this. Or "I *guarantee* this will work for you."

4. **Health.** Obviously, most people care more about their health than about money. For good reason. If we lose our money, we can get it back. Regaining health is much more difficult. So why not make health part of the negotiation process? For example, you could say, "This will produce a *healthy* return." Or, "If we can reach an agreement on this, it will be *healthy* for us both."

5. **Love.** Many industries play upon the appeal of love, including the wine and alcoholic beverage industries, florists, and candy makers. Online dating services are today's matchmakers—a multimillion dollar business based on helping people find love.

   In a negotiation, you could say, "You are going to *love* this!" Or "All of my clients *love* this!"

6. **Money.** Most people would have trouble paying off an unexpected bill of $1,000. Many are only thirty days away from

bankruptcy. You can bet that money ranks among the top three on this list. Money can be used to negotiate anything. "You will make a lot of *money* with this idea." Or, "We are talking about real *money* for you right now!"

7. **New.** In the United States, we have a strange preference for anything new. We want state-of-the-art, cutting-edge products and services. We cast away major items such as used cars and computers after short periods of time. We call them obsolete whether they work or not. We always want the latest model, the newest design.

    Using this concept in negotiation: "Here is a *new* idea that will work for you!" Or, "You will like this idea. Not many people know about it because it is so *new*!"

8. **Proven.** Americans have a strong desire to avoid the unproven and unreliable. We want products are proven, so we won't have to take a risk. For example, "This idea has been *proven* to work!" Or, "It is *proven* to work with hundreds of my clients!"

9. **Results.** The quickest way to get attention in a negotiation is to let the other side know that what you offer will be a benefit. It will produce results and have an impact. "If we can list your house, you will get *results*. We do things no other Realtors do! We get *results*."

10. **Safety.** Closely linked to health, safety is a characteristic of products that most people take for granted. But more and

more, safety grabs attention. For example, "I know that *safety* for you and your family is important." "Let's make this *safe* for you." "Many of my clients negotiate *safe* money concepts, *safe* investments, and even *safe* tax strategies."

11. **Save.** Americans love discounts. They love getting a deal few others get. Even a deal that will not help them make money must at least help them save money. It's like someone who saves money on something they didn't even need. For example, "I can *save* you 35 percent if we can do this deal today!" Or, "I would love to *save* you some money. Can we make a deal on this?"

12. **You.** This word is peppered throughout this book. *You* is one of the most soothing words to anyone's ear. The other, even more attractive, word is your negotiation partner's own name.

These words will help you put more persuasive zing into everything you say, advertise and write. Use them in websites, social media, and even email blasts. When you use them during a phone conversation, you'll cause your listener to become more intent on your message. These words will rivet attention on whatever idea you're proposing.

5

Conclusion

The constant theme of this book is that we all negotiate all the time. Whether you are scheduling an appointment, trying to agree on a vacation spot this summer, or buying a car, you are negotiating daily.

What makes the process of negotiation challenging is the way we communicate. We don't feel comfortable negotiating because we don't listen or present ideas based on what we hear. Negotiation tactics don't work well if we don't know how to use people skills in applying them.

The other challenge is that most of us have never been taught how to negotiate. We may know what we want, but don't know how to get it. There is no structure; much of time we are just winging it. Sometimes we got a deal, and other times we didn't, but we certainly don't have a system. This book has provided you a system to use in getting anything you want.

The other challenge to negotiating effectively is your mind-set. We think of negotiation often as demeaning or embarrassing. We think of asking for a better deal as insulting to the other side. Would you be more reluctant to negotiate with a friend of stranger? Both could give you a deal if you knew what to say. Both would probably like to do business with you. Both should be treated with respect and elegance. You don't have to be adversarial. Negotiation can be both friendly and fun.

We often tend to think that a printed price is sacrosanct. My wife, Merita, thinks negotiation is embarrassing. She will walk away from a price that is too expensive. That is a lost sale to a vendor. I am likely to ask polite questions to determine if the other side wants to make a deal. A price is only what two sides can agree on. Otherwise, it is simply a dream or a guess. If there is no agreement, the printed price means nothing. Most sellers would love to negotiate rather than miss a sales opportunity. They feel that a sale including a concession is better than no sale at all.

We have also emphasized that a negotiated deal is the most amount of hourly income you will ever make. If you can get a discount of $1,000 from a one-hour negotiation, doesn't that mean you've earned $1,000 per hour? How many activities have you engaged in that earn you $1,000 from a single hour of effort? Bill Gates made more than $100 billion from a single negotiation on a software operating system that he didn't even own. George Lucas earned more than $1 billion just because he was unwilling to accept a $200,000 fee for directing and producing the first episode of *Star Wars*. The examples go on and on. The better you can negotiate, the more income you will earn. To become a good negotiator, you need to practice these skills.

In chapter 1, you learned negotiation strategies and skills. You learned to never jump at the first offer. Why? Because you might just get a better one. You also learned that money is not the only concession available. There are many other areas that a negotiation could produce. These include delivery, speed of service, extended warranty, and even extra services. Don't think that money is the only way to do a deal. There are many other areas that are profitable.

Many people don't choose to negotiate because of fear. One of the most difficult fears to overcome is your natural fear of rejection. Nobody likes to hear no. There's a feeling of embarrassment and loss of self-esteem. But you've learned some interesting ways of hearing no less often. You've learned how to gain compliance. For example, you learned how to strategically use the word *because*.

Next, you learned to ask for more than you expect to get. Why? Because you just might get it. You also learned to use rejection, then retreat. This is when the other side says no, but instead of giving up and ending the negotiation, you retreat to a lesser deal.

Bracketing is a way of deciding on the price you want to pay, then making an offer that produces a compromise in the middle. For example, if you want to pay $16 and the seller wants $18, your counteroffer would be $14. This works because of our natural tendency to split the difference. Poor negotiators are usually quick to reach a fast compromise. That is usually a suggestion to split the difference.

Flinching is a nonverbal way to show your displeasure or disagreement to an offer. You learned how to appropriately flinch, causing the other side to make a quick concession. It's important not to show too much enthusiasm in any negotiation. If the other side senses too much acceptance, they may add on costs and ask you to make concessions.

We discussed why you should never offer to split the difference. The reason is that splitting the difference might never end. You should never offer to split the difference, because the other side may ask many more times. This could continue until you have no profit left.

The vise is a great way to gain immediate concessions. The request is simple. Say, "You will have to do better than that," and wait for a response. Often the other side will make a better offer. Sometimes they will ask how much better they have to do, causing you to make a counteroffer.

When you are faced with the good cop, bad cop tactic, avoid thinking the good cop is on your side. They are both colluding against you. Ask to speak directly to the bad cop.

Never change your offer except in response to a counter. Otherwise you have diminished your negotiation position. The other side may think you are desperate and will try to get larger concessions.

Nibbling is a great way to gain concessions after an agreement is reached. You can make small gains by nibbling at the end—or lose profits by allowing them. If you get nibbled, ask for a concession in return. The other side will stop nibbling your profits away.

You can set up a faster, easier negotiation by setting up for yes. This is done by finding out the other side's pressure to get the deal done. You can also set up a faster yes by being both charming and appealing to their ego. Confrontational tactics rarely work.

In chapter 2, "Easy Tactics You Need to Learn," you found out why you should never make the first offer. This is a very important starting place in any negotiation. It's critical never to accept the first offer, but also to get the other side to make the first offer. A good negotiator will probably start high, hoping you will make a counter offer. But there are very few good negotiators. With a little persistence and discipline, you will be able to get most people to make the first offer.

When we discussed the concept of declining value of services, you learned that the favors, concession, and extra benefits you provide are soon diminished, devalued, and forgotten. If you plan to provide extras, make sure their value is negotiated up front. Not after the service is rendered.

Dumb is always smart in any negotiation. Making assumptions may be hazardous. Act as though you want total clarity throughout any discussion. Even though you think you have an agreement, repeat everything back to make sure. The last thing you want is a misunderstanding in any part of a negotiated deal.

We've also discussed the written agreement. It's important not only to read every change in the whole agreement, but to write it. If you are the one creating the written agreement, there will be no surprises. But if any changes are made, read the whole agreement, not just the individual areas of change. You may be stuck with a bad deal that you didn't review.

When we spoke about the decreasing value of concessions, we mentioned how the other side will take concessions for granted but will also devalue them later. You can also make a negotiation progress faster by making each concession progressively smaller. This will cause the other side to realize that any further discussion will result in diminishing returns.

When we spoke about the red herring, you learned that negotiating for an item that you don't want will give you valuable information on getting a deal for the item you do want. For example, negotiating for a car model similar to the one you want and walking away will give you a good idea of the bottom line on the model you do want to buy. There is no downside to using this technique, since there is no obligation to buy or reach an agreement.

We also spoke about how to force a decision. You can do this by paying close attention to the pressure the other site is under. Perhaps they have deadlines. Perhaps they need to meet a quota. Perhaps there is competition pressure from another vendor, who has offered a better deal. The way to force a decision is to listen very intently and ask questions.

Monopoly money is a gimmick that negotiators use to diminish the impact of any cost. They make an offer of a cost of $3 per day, disguising the higher price total of $90 a month. They assume you will not notice the difference between an extended warranty of $1,200 per year or the cost of a cup of Starbucks coffee per day. This funny money is a way of reframing your emotions about money into accepting their higher-priced offer. Never fall for this approach.

When we discussed requests for proposals (RFPs), you learned to always talk verbally to the party making the request. Don't text. Don't email. Just talk. Never respond with only a written offer. There is a lot more to an RFP than just price. It is also good to assume that your chances of doing a deal without a verbal conversation are minimal. The decision parameters are usually not just about price. There is a difference between price and cost. There may be other needs involved in the request you don't know about.

The higher authority tactic is used by the other side to get approval from a committee. But you can also use the higher authority to your own benefit. Simply let the other side know that you need approval. Your way around their higher authority is to speak to the person making the decision. Don't negotiate a deal with someone who can't say yes. We also learned in this section about the up-front close. This is asking the other side for a yes or no answer before you make a presentation or offer.

We discussed whether you can walk away from a deal. Are you so attached that you need it at all costs? Or are you prepared to walk away from a deal that is not right? You will never know the best price or the greatest concessions you can get unless you walk away. The great news is, you can always walk back in and get the same offer. Sometimes we get so involved in completing a negotiation that we make bad deals. Most great negotiators walk away from ten times more deals than they accept. The best way to learn when to walk away is to gain experience and negotiate more often.

Sometimes you will hear the other side make a take it or leave it demand. When you hear this kind of statement, it's often from somebody who can't make a decision. Ask for the name of the person who can. Also probe as to why this statement is made. Most people can be abrupt and inappropriate when told to do something by a superior. Find out who the person is and engage them directly.

The hot potato tactic is often used by the other side to get you to solve their problems. They throw up an objection, expecting you to either make concessions or fix the issue. Never fall for this tactic. Always turn it back towards them. For example, say, "What's the best way for you to fix this?" Don't let their problem become yours. Don't accept responsibility for their challenges. Make them fix their own problems.

In chapter 3, "Advanced Negotiation Techniques," we focused on areas of negotiation besides tactics and strategies. They can help your negotiations progress more quickly and lead to the outcomes you want.

Technique number one was how to handle tough negotiations. We spoke reluctant buyers and sellers. A buyer who appears too anxious is often unable to gain the concessions they want. A seller who is overly interested may make too many concessions to an uninterested party. Many buyers who appear mildly interested gain the greatest concessions, because they seem more likely to walk away. Many sellers who seem nonchalant may also ask for fewer concessions than those who seem desperate.

The next technique we discussed was to stay calm during any negotiation and avoid any level of confrontation. Any time the negotiation moves from respectful conversation to contentious disagreement, you are unlikely to get the outcome you want. People dig in when they become emotional. When you find yourself in this kind of situation (even a disagreement in your marriage), walk away and take a break. You can always reengage when you both feel more relaxed.

We also spoke about resorting to a committee. Like the higher authority, a committee is only a roadblock to getting the deal you want. It's much better to find out who is running the committee and making direct contact with them. Remember, don't negotiate with people who cannot say yes. But it's always good to retain your own committee, if you have one.

We've discussed how to use these negotiation tactics in dealing with customer complaints. Surprisingly, customers and clients who never have problems are minimally likely to refer business to you. But those who have complaints that are happily and successfully resolved are twelve times more likely to stay loyal and refer business to you, according to one Harvard University study.

Getting good at resolving complaints should be a priority in your business. This skill revolves around making people feel heard and asking what they want as quickly in the conversation as possible. You can always negotiate a solution later. Most customers feel they have to argue to gain resolution. Simply agree with them immediately and ask what they would like to see happen. Then negotiate.

The next skill was one of the most important in this book: how to listen. Many experts discus how important listening skills are, but never tell you specifically how to use them.

In this chapter, you also learned how to use the five-step bridge. You learned how to gain three needs, recap like a psychotherapist, and trial-close to gain a commitment to a solution. The bridge is arguably the most important communication skill you will ever use. In one study, it was shown that 83 percent of negotiations succeed because the other side feels understood. Only 6 percent succeed because the other side was made to understand.

Every negotiator uses a mental strategy in making a decision. We discussed the notion that people really don't change. Your basic personality was developed between the age of two and seven years old. We can learn, adapt, and develop, but who you are and how you think is unlikely to change. We focused this section on finding out how the negotiator made decisions in the past. They are likely to use the same strategy in the future.

We also learned the "let's assume" technique. This is putting the other side a year in the future and working backwards, telling us what a successful negotiation looks like. This is an amazingly successful tool in finding out what the other side wants. Once you discover this, you know exactly what a win-win negotiation looks like to them. You can either walk away or negotiate a deal that works for you both.

In the last section, we discussed how to overcome negotiation objections. We discussed the four reasons why people object. These are rarely about money. We then discussed the nine steps of overcoming even the toughest objections. The biggest objection block is always the stall. Many people will say they want take some time to think about it, but that really means wasting your time. Even a no is better than making you chase them. To avoid the stall, we discussed how to use the up-front close. In other words, say yes, say no, but don't say maybe.

Chapter 4 was on psychological techniques you can use when negotiating. Rarely do people negotiate in a bubble. We are all human beings and communicate through emotion and logic, but those communication modes are 87 percent nonverbal. Reading body language will help you gain much more successful outcomes, because you are communicating much more successfully.

We discussed extensively how important trust is in any negotiation. Without trust, you wouldn't accept a dollar on the streets of New York City. With trust, you would do business on a handshake.

We talked about how to gain trust by matching and mirroring. If the other person speaks slowly, you should also. If they speed up their verbal pace, you should increase yours as well. Nonverbal matching is equally important. Trust comes more quickly with those we find similar to us. Trust takes longer with those whose behavior we can't predict. This means, for example, if they sit back in a chair, you should sit back in yours. If they lean forward, after twenty seconds you should lean forward also.

Learning the other side's keywords and phrases will also help you in any negotiation. If the other side uses a particular phrase, try to use those keywords back to them. For example, if a car seller describes their vehicle as a "cherry," use that word as well. If I describe myself as a business psychologist instead of a motivational speaker, a good negotiator would refer to me as a business psychologist too.

We went on to discuss how to spot when the other side is telling the truth. In any negotiation, it is critical to determine whether or not you are being lied to. A good police investigator is able to interview people and spot inconsistencies in their story in order to solve the crime. We spoke about discovering whether somebody is lying or telling the truth by the way they move their eyes.

Since rapport and trust are so critical in any negotiation, we also discussed a psychological concept called *proxemics*. This is the study of personal space. Someone who makes you stand or sit three feet away is showing a level of distrust. We call this the *stranger distance*. On the other hand, people who sit or stand within one to two feet of you are showing the greatest amount of trust and rapport you will ever have. Often you can just feel it. But is also good to see rapport and trust as well by noticing the way they sit and stand.

Because it's so important to push people at the right time and back off appropriately, we discussed the concept of stress cues. These are the nonverbal signals people use when they feel stressed, pushed, or pressed. It's important to recognize these cues, because we never want people to feel pushed. But we do want to be assertive enough to progress the negotiation quickly. We don't want to push. But how would you know when people are feeling pushed? This section showed you what to look for.

We then moved on to buying signals. People will show you what they are thinking long before they tell you. When the other side shows you a buying signal, they have accepted your idea. If you don't recognize these cues, you may oversell and buy it back. One of these cues is when the negotiator leans forward. But it could mean the person is only fidgeting.

We discussed how to calibrate the other side. This means to get a baseline reading in the first ten minutes, and then compare any later nonverbal cues to that initial baseline behavior.

The last section provided the most persuasive words you can use in presenting your message. You should use them in any negotiation you undertake—on your website, business card, LinkedIn profile, or any other message you want people to retain.

As we have discussed earlier, this is the first book on the mechanics of negotiation, as well as the psychology behind it. Many previous books have presented ideas on how to negotiate more effectively. But any negotiation is not only about skills and tactics. It is about how you communicate, read emotions, listen, and present.

If you use these techniques and concepts within twenty-four hours of learning them, you will reach more effective outcomes in any negotiation than ever before. We all negotiate, all the time. It's shocking that most of us have never had formal training in these skills. You will use them every day. As you learn and practice, your abilities will far outshine those of any others you negotiate with.